10/09

"An in   ritual
awakeni   time
it relates   savor
each cha

                                                           nough

"Blazir   ansfor-
mation,   dition
to the g   Mayan
Calenda   ig the
best of t   unt of
consciou

                                                         n Your
                                                         raveler

"The   arche-
typal   and
poetic   s personal   teller,
and h   ation
will d   ights
of ins

                                                         n the
                                                         Mind

"The call of a mourning dove spurs Daniel's magical journey in which the real promise of the Mayan Prophecy gradually comes to light. Jock Whitehouse, inventively mixing chronologies and cultures, provides Daniel with Leila the Teacher, Melchior the Shaman, and a small brown and gray snake to guide him on his way to the Ledge of Quetzal. Here he comes full circle to a deep recognition of the dove's message. This is the way the universe is. A divine reality, comprehensible to us all, is present already and always."

—Ann Jauregui, PhD, author of *Epiphanies: Where Science & Miracles Meet* and winner of 2008 Nautilus Book Award

"Simple, lyrical, and profound. Unfolds like a dream-vision and leaves you with the feeling you have been visited by the spirit of a future which calls us to oneness and authentic spiritual liberation."

—James O'Dea, visionary activist, fellow and former president of IONS, and writer and lecturer on global transformation and the 2012 era

THE
LEDGE OF
QUETZAL
-BEYOND 2012

THE LEDGE OF QUETZAL – BEYOND 2012

A Magical Adventure to Discover the Real
Promise of the Mayan Prophecy

Jock Whitehouse

Illustrations by Tom Knapp

WEISER BOOKS
San Francisco, CA / Newburyport, MA

First published in 2009 by
Red Wheel/Weiser, LLC
With offices at:
500 Third Street, Suite 230
San Francisco, CA 94107
www.redwheelweiser.com

ISBN: 978-1-57863-459-0
Library of Congress Cataloging-in-Publication Data
available upon request.

Cover design by Donna Linden
Text design by Mary Beth Fiorentino
Typeset in Adobe Garamond

Printed in the United States of America
TS
10 9 8 7 6 5 4 3 2 1

♻ Text paper contains a minimum of
30% post-consumer-waste material.

To my beloved wife Deborah,
for sharing the journey with me.

The canyon of the eagle.

Preface

WE KNOW WHO WE ARE.

We have stood at the edge of the canyon reaching, reaching beyond our selves to touch once again the eternal. Below, the stream flows deeper and deeper into the earth while, on the far side, the cave dwellings of our ancestors are cut in sunlight and shadow. Above them, a vast vertical outcrop has been poured over with the elemental stain of eons passing. At the horizon, smooth rim rock breasts up against the sky. Ancient footpaths lace down through cleft rock, and still, warm winds whisper through the cottonwoods. Our hearts once knew all the secrets of this place and spoke its timeless language. But we left so long ago. Now we have come back all this way—isolated, mute, filled with hunger to be reborn. From nowhere, an immense golden eagle glides not thirty feet overhead and disappears. For an instant, time opens and we can see infinitely into our selves.

We return to our cities pierced from within.

I

"I'VE HAD A VISION," DANIEL SAID TO HIS GUIDES.

The guides stirred within him.

"The vision I've had is that we are all divine."

After days of walking and climbing, Daniel was high in the mountains of tropical Mexico. Early morning clouds and mist enveloped him like a shell of pearl. Trees dripped with moisture and the smell of wet soil rose up along the path. High above, beyond seeing, the chilling call of a *chachalaca* led the way. Daniel was in the company of his guides, who spoke to him with one voice from within. He was on the last days of a journey to the high ledge where the god Quetzal would appear before him. There, he was to receive the final realization of his being.

He had climbed and climbed up into the clouds since before dawn. As he left the village below, Daniel could see in the faint first light of day a small brown and gray snake moving through the grass by the side of the road. Possessed for an instant by total understanding, he picked up the snake gently and fed it into his shirt and around his waist. He could feel it tightening against his skin. Now his sandals were soaked through, chafing his feet. "Do I really belong here?" he wondered, still astonished at how much had happened and how far he had come. To him, this was the land of innocent Indians who went to church, planted corn, and ushered kindling-laden burros along steep hillside paths—of mystical shamans who used peyote, made sacrifices, and did crazed dances in the smoke of the gods.

Through all these years, the guides had led him from his home in the United States to this remote place of transformation. It had been a journey through some of the darkest valleys he had ever known, a journey whose purpose was often revealed through the power of epiphany.

Already, warm air had begun to rise up from the valley, urging the mist before it, but Daniel didn't want the mist to leave. It embraced him and the trees and stones and the mountain, and he felt comforted by its moisture, by the sounds it carried and the smells it awakened. He wanted to breathe in its wholeness. The feeling reminded him of times when he yearned to be joined with all his surroundings—joined in a oneness he couldn't touch. Now, in this instant, he was bathed in it.

The path grew steeper as he ascended. He leaned on his staff and small stones skidded out from under his feet. He looked down and saw his white skin smeared with mud and marveled again that he was in sandals. This was a land of origins and simple things. A land of sandals. He had allowed himself to be drawn into the unfamiliar in order to be transformed. But a part of him feared how terrifying the transformation could become. The bird beckoned ahead. From time to time, his guides spoke to him, urging him to pause, to feel the power of his surroundings. Close to his ears, he heard droplets of dew fall from the trees and pelt the impermeable shell of his jacket. He felt the steepness of the climb and the weight of the pack on his back and he was out of breath.

A number of days ago, when he began this part of his journey, there had been times in the early morning and after sundown when he could barely see the path a few feet before him—a path marked by traces of dark ground occasionally bounded by rocks and grasses and the bare roots of trees. Sometimes the path simply vanished, enveloped in the dimensional whisper of air through pine needles. Where was the heart to follow? The sounds? The dampness?

The darkness that covered his eyes? He had to allow his guides to move him through the ferns and around large boulders to find his way once again. In the beginning, years ago, it had always been frightening to let his guides take over, because he had been so utterly lost and knew how lost he could again become. *Trust,* the guides had said. And each time they led him through darkness into light, his trust grew.

He remembered only a few nights earlier climbing a long path in the dark, up the hill to where the ceremony had taken place. It was a flat, charred piece of ground. There, in the glow of two large fires, he had looked into obsidian eyes, seen dark painted faces, felt their hands all over his body, their hair on his back, and touched their bare feet stomping among coals in the dust. Amid the dancing and the noise, the priest Bartolomeo, a small, frail man, suddenly stepped from the darkness into the light of the fires holding his hands apart. The people became silent. Two women gently pulled Daniel down to his knees before an altar, then knelt on either side of him. A pair of hands rested on his shoulders.

When all was still—as still as the incense that hung in the air—the priest came to him and placed three fingers on his left wrist. He felt his heart begin to pound uncontrollably. Then the priest touched both of his temples. After a suspenseful silence, the priest intoned, *"Susto,"* and a murmur of affirmation swept in from the glow of the fires. For the first time, Daniel noticed that a cross made from grass had been planted atop a small mound of earth that formed the altar. Small flowers were strewn about and candles burned around the front edge of the mound. A tall dish at the center held the smoldering *copal.* The women beside him began to moan from deep within their throats. They patted their thighs, then put their hands together in a form of prayer with their index fingers folded inward. They patted their thighs once again. The priest held a bouquet of *albahaca,* a white carnation, a thin branch from a pepper tree, and a large specked egg. One of the men held a cup to the priest's lips and the priest sipped. Then the priest turned and from his mouth sprayed both the bouquet and Daniel's face with the clear liquid. It felt hot and smelled of sour, fermenting plants.

The priest began to grunt with short breaths and passed the bouquet over Daniel's head, then brushed down his front and back, making sweeping motions over his entire body. The moans from the women beside him grew mournful as they grabbed handfuls of dirt and threw them into the air. When the priest had swept even the soles of Daniel's bare feet, he placed the bouquet to the left of the altar and broke the egg into a glass of water. Then he took up another bouquet from the right side of the altar, this one with a red carnation, and yet another egg. Again the priest sipped from a cup held to his lips and spat the fermented juice onto the bouquet and onto Daniel. He could feel the closeness of the priest's body leaning over his own and the heat and grunting of the priest's sour breath.

After what seemed an extended tunnel of time, the priest laid his hand upon Daniel's head and, looking up into the dark heavens, released a long, mournful howl that reverberated from his reedy frame. The women on either side of Daniel took him by the shoulders and shook him violently back and forth and from side to side. Then they went to the altar and each withdrew long strands of grass from the cross and wrapped them around Daniel's wrists and around his head. The priest had now broken the last egg into a second glass of water and was gazing intently through the sides of both glasses. He came to Daniel holding the two glasses before him for Daniel to see. *"Su susto,"* the priest said. In each glass, the whites and the golden yolks, magnified by the water, formed deep symmetrical swirls shot through with burning reflections of the flames that filled the night. Daniel saw the milky threads of his fright that had been cleansed from him. And through the water his fright gazed back at him with the glowing yellow eyes of a great cat.

Looking up into the heavens, the priest
released a long, mournful howl.

Now with his guides on the mountainside, he suddenly felt like crying. He stopped. He felt as if he were being taken up into a realm that knew all his secret yearnings—a place that could hold his heart in a light he had never known. In preparation for his journey, the voice that spoke to him when he died told him that, before reaching the ledge of Quetzal, he would experience levels of recollection and realization along the way. Already many levels had been awakened within him. At each one he had stepped outside of time to assimilate the great truth being offered him. They were all similar, and yet different in very important ways. Now, on the verge of crying, there was a part of him that didn't want to move on, but rather wanted to linger here at this edge of becoming, teasing himself with the possibility of total dissolution.

His body surged with energy. The snake felt the energy and stirred for a moment. His arms and shoulders and heart felt full. There seemed to be a force of incredible love rising up from the mountain. He put his hand on the peeling bark of a tree. This is a holy place, he felt. He wanted to give himself to it, to dissolve into the soil and into all his surroundings. His calves ached from the climb, but the pain felt as if it belonged.

This was not a place without contrasts. There were pockets of great suffering left by those who had come before him, and the mixture of suffering and love awakened in him a feeling of compassion. He wanted to merge with it. Living and dying seemed to be the same. Without warning, he burst into tears and laughter, holding the small pouch that hung from his neck as if to steady himself.

Soon, through the trees a few yards down from the edge of the path, he noticed a small pyramid of stones—like an altar, perhaps waist high—that had been mounded up on a piece of ground that seemed to have been cleared and smoothed over for this purpose. As he moved toward it, he saw that a bundle of twigs wrapped in a vine and flanked by two small circles of ashes and charred wood had been placed before the pyramid. "I'm not the only one who feels the power of this mid-way place," he said to himself. "This is a place of preparation."

He crossed his legs and sat before the stones, hands resting palms up on his knees, facing west. Eyes closed, he breathed in deeply to relax his body and drain the churning from his mind. Moist air flowed up around his neck and face. Soon, his breathing settled into a deep and pendular rhythm, and the shell of his awareness extended outward an arm's length beyond his skin. Amid all the sounds and textures of the mountain, he began to find stillness. With the ledge only a half day ahead, for long moments, moments without time, he allowed himself to *be,* preparing himself to receive. Here, high on this rapturous mountain, he would soon touch the largest truth of his life.

He had come such a long, long way.

2

THERE WAS A TIME WHEN DANIEL SEEMED VERY HAPPY. HE HAD A wife and children, more than enough money, everything he could possibly want. They lived in a beautiful countryside of rolling green hills, farms with barns and tractors, sheep, dairy cows, and restored old stone houses that spoke of hand-made things when people lived close to the earth. He never mixed with his neighbors. They were farmers and he was a businessman who commuted each day to work. Around his house there were tall oak trees and maples whose leaves turned to brilliant red, yellow, and orange in the fall. Narrow roads were laid out like gray ribbons over the land, their edges defined by pastures and fields of corn and wheat, and fences made from stones. In winter, those same roads became like streams of snow meandering through stubbled fields.

For many years he thought the work he did was important, and that was enough to please him. He had a relaxed manner and got along with everyone. He was able to bring people together and elicit the best from them. Many thought he was headed for the top. He, however, never felt such ambitions, and so he didn't think much about it. Advancements came easily and, if he made it to the top, then so be it.

What he did think was that, even though he enjoyed his work—even loved his work—there was always something missing. Sometimes at night, when he went out to close the garage door, or when he carried the garbage out to the road for early-morning pickup, he looked up into the starlit heavens and felt devastated. It was all so beautiful, so serene, so balanced and complete. There in the night, instead of going back inside to his family, he sometimes walked up to a lushly mown knoll and just lay down, looking up into the infinite sky. So many feelings came over him in these moments—weakness, sadness, emptiness, helplessness. More than anything, and for as long as he could remember, he had wanted to become one with the great panorama that, in those moments, enveloped him. He could not have known then the depth of his yearning or how dramatically its power would change his life.

One afternoon at lunch he asked a friend, "Don't you feel there's more to life than just this?" The friend laughed. "Lots of people feel that way, but not for long," he said. "It's a dangerous thought. It leads to unhappiness. Besides, look how full your life is." The answer made him uneasy.

Not long after that, driving to work, he realized that, for quite some time, perhaps a couple of times a year, he had caught flashing visions of people as empty bodies. They moved around, worked on things that weren't important, and made a fuss about things that had no meaning at all. Beneath that, he saw their aloneness and helplessness—and beneath that, he saw their fear. There, he saw them as children inflicted with great pain. That vision seemed real, much more real than what they had become as adults. The visions were just bursts across his awareness that disappeared as quickly as they appeared.

"Look at mankind," he sometimes said to himself. "Then look at the universe. What are we doing? What am *I* doing?" The thought made him feel momentarily lost and anxious. Then he just forgot about it. And for a long, long time now, he had forgotten about it. Then—each quite suddenly, although years apart—his life, his work, and his health began to change.

One September evening as he came home from work, his wife met him on the porch. Two packed suitcases stood beside her. "I'm leaving you," she said. Just a week earlier they had dropped their youngest child off at college, and now his wife was saying goodbye. For a long moment, he couldn't understand what was happening. It was as if a wave of scorching air had suddenly rolled through to suck his breath away. Fire rose up from within him, and then he began to rage. "How can you do this? How can you do this?" He waved his arms and strode through the house. "How can you *do* this?"

By nightfall she was gone. Alone in the house, the waves of anger receded and in the darkness lay bare a wound whose depth and richness would take ten years to explore.

The first nights were filled with long hours of chaos. Daniel was enveloped in an emptiness that seemed to expand infinitely outward. Sensations surged through him and over him—first one and then another, each pure, of one substance, and paralyzing. The tumult was everywhere, flowing over his skin, inside his chest and throat, in the distant sound of a barking dog. There was nothing by which he could orient himself. He was drowning in darkness. He lay in the middle of his bed, large, empty, cold, yet soaked in sweat. Every creak in the house was magnified. Sleep, instead of smothering him into itself, lingered over him, pierced again and again by the realization of what had happened. And when there was sleep, it became a twisted nightmare. He was ushered into a landscape of geometric shapes that didn't fit, a nauseating repetition of equations that didn't equate, endless searches for something he couldn't define. Once awake, his logic broke apart. The structure of his mind seemed to crumble. He was in psychological free fall.

He knew no coherent thoughts at times like these, only unfamiliar visitors that bathed him in the hot and cold of their breath. His arms, throat, and shoulders became conduits for fear, leading directly to his heart. Any lightness and grace he had known seemed to have been driven from his experience, and he wouldn't recognize their absence for months to come. And always, there was a chronic, gnarled hunger in his stomach.

He had never felt so helpless. In spite of his nearly fifty years, he could find nothing he believed in strongly enough to hold on to. This sense of separateness from the universe would take years to heal. Now the darkness opened up beneath him, and it was vast and bottomless. Late on that first night, he dreamed that his body was a massive piece of coal and he awakened to throw up. He had no idea what was happening to him, and happening in such large denominations.

What he felt happening to him was a violation of everything he believed. His family was breaking up in the face of solemn vows to the contrary. In his heritage, divorce was never an option. Now a cloak of decay and impermanence hung over everything he saw.

Nighttime and sleep rolled like a ship in a storm. His dreams were contortions of the real and the unreal, beyond what his mind could grasp. He was experiencing his first conscious encounter with an unknown part of himself and he could find no horizon.

What's more, he was blind to the scale of isolation that engulfed him. Instead of feeling embraced by the universe, a creature of its creation, he stood alone against an immense and impersonal void with nothing more to hold on to than his meager self. When crisis came, it stripped away the familiar and opened a vast wilderness of the unknown. Relationships, proportion, balance, sanity—all seemed like structures from a distorted dream. Whatever had worked in the past suddenly seemed to fall apart; he struggled to form a new cosmic order.

By some alchemy of profound psychological pain, during these dark nights, the man Daniel had been began to dissolve from within. The structure of his thinking was dismantled. The truths he had clung to, the beliefs that paralyzed his imagination, started to fall away. Of all the rigid rules he had carefully built up over a lifetime, there remained only an amorphous imperative he no longer recognized. The person he had been, died. In his place was a child about to be born—tender, needing to be held, needing to trust the goodness of the world into which it would emerge.

The change was profound—the acid in his stomach drawn to a thread of sweetness he had barely begun to taste. Though deep in darkness, something great stirred within him, inviting him ever so persuasively to reach forward and embrace the unknown. His life was being transformed, and he knew it.

SEVERAL MONTHS LATER, DANIEL TOOK A WALK BY HIMSELF through fields not far from his home. It was a bright spring afternoon. Farms were being pulled back into shape from the winter. Barn doors were left open, cows were turned loose into still-soggy pastures, and the first green blades of wheat poked through the earth. His own flower beds were still untended from the fall, the grass too young and wet to be mowed. He had walked two hills over from his house and down toward a stand of sycamores and willows that lined a stream. There, he heard what sounded like the desperate bleating of a lamb. He was near a farm that he knew raised sheep; perhaps one of them had been injured.

As he came to a crooked barbed-wire fence that separated him from the stream, he saw a small lamb up to its belly in mud on the far side of the stream. It cried and cried. He wasn't used to farm animals. He wasn't dressed for farm work. Still, he looked for a place in the fence where he could climb over. On the other side, he felt his boots sink into the mud along the banks of the stream. As he stood on a stepping stone in mid-stream, his soles slick with mud, his foot flew out from under him. The icy water bit into his chest and shoulders. His hip hit a rock. The lamb cried out.

Dazed, he began to pull himself up. Water filled his pants and weighed heavily in his wool shirt. Gradually, he slogged to the far bank and, looking up, saw a large silhouetted figure in a broad-brimmed hat striding over the crest of the hill toward him.

A great coat billowed out behind him and he seemed to be carrying a rifle. "What are you doing on my land?!" the figure demanded. "What are you doing with my sheep?" Soon the figure was upon him, the shotgun leveled at his chest.

The dark figure strode toward Daniel carrying a shotgun.

"Are you Mr. Schneider?" Daniel asked, staring at the two barrels pointing toward him.

"I know who I am. Who are you?"

"I'm your neighbor from over the hill, on Stoltz Road," he said. Now his shoulder began to hurt and his feet sloshed in his boots. "I was trying to rescue your lamb from the mud."

The farmer seemed to soften. "Looks t'me like you're the one need'n rescue," he said. Up close, he was a huge man with a deep, husky voice. "Here, hold this," he said, handing over his shotgun. Then he sidled a few steps down the bank and, in one smooth movement, wrapped his arms around the bleating lamb, hauled it from the mud, and set it on higher ground. "When I heard all the commotion, I thought you were one of the neighbor's dogs after my sheep." The lamb stood motionless, looking up the hill. "The dogs come over here and just eat the guts out of my sheep. The other day I found one of my lambs all torn up, so I just picked her up, took 'er over to Geiger's, pounded on the door, and when Geiger opened up I just threw the dead lamb at him, blood, guts, and everything. Next time, I'll shoot his dogs and throw *them* at him." The farmer looked Daniel over as he took back his gun. "Looks like you could use some drying out," he said and, with his head, gestured toward his house over the hill.

They crested the hill together and on the other side came to a large stone barn and, standing between two wide maples, the Schneider farmhouse. Daniel's side ached and he could feel himself starting to shiver. "C'mon in," the farmer said, kicking his boots off on the back porch. Daniel had to sit on a bench to unlace his boots and pull off his muddy socks. He entered the house barefoot and cold. "Leila, I think we've found your man," the farmer called.

The house smelled of smoke. Massive wood beams braced the ceiling. A walk-in fireplace filled the far end of the room. On a low table in front of the couch, a single yellow crocus floated in a bowl of water. Daniel heard the creaking of stairs and soon Leila appeared through a small doorway. She was her husband's opposite: frail, graceful, with olive skin and deep brown eyes. Gray streaked through her dark hair, which was pulled back in a bun. She didn't seem to be a farming wife.

"I found him down by the creek trying to pull one of the lambies out of the mud," the farmer said, hanging his hat and coat on a peg beside the door. "He's the one who lives on the old Yerger farm." Turning to Daniel, he asked, "What'd you say your name was?"

"I'm Dan Bancroft. I didn't mean to barge in on you this way. I apologize. I'm a mess," he said, shaking his head. "I fell in the stream."

The woman moved toward Daniel and offered him a slender hand. "I'm Leila Schneider," she said in a soft voice. "There's no need to apologize." She reached out and touched his arm. "My, you're soaked clear through," she said. "Karl, don't you think some of Jake's things would fit him? They're about the same size. Jake is our youngest son. He's in Texas wildcatting, so I don't think he'll mind if you borrow some of his things for a while," the woman said. "Here, come with me." She led him through the kitchen and down a narrow hallway to Jake's room.

Trophies lined the windowsills of the room and posters of race drivers and soccer players hung from the walls. The woman laid out a plaid shirt, a pair of blue jeans, and socks from a dresser drawer. Then she reached behind the door. "Here's a towel. Bring your things out with you and I'll put them in the dryer."

Daniel emptied his pockets onto the dresser, pulled off his wet clothes, put them in a pile by the door, and dried off. His hip was red and aching, and he could see in the mirror that the skin on his left shoulder had been scraped raw. It stung as he threaded his arm into the shirt. The pants were too tight around the waist, but they'd do. He stopped to look at himself in the mirror and, for a long moment, wondered what he was doing here. He tried to smooth out his hair with his hand. And what was that remark the farmer had made: "We've found your man"?

When he rejoined them in the kitchen, Leila took his wet clothes and promptly disappeared down a narrow stairwell into the basement. Late afternoon sun filled the room.

"We're boiling some water for tea," the farmer said. "Have a seat." Now his voice was like a whisper, part sound and part breath—as if it had been exhaled from between two membranes deep in his chest. A cup, saucer, and spoon had been set on the kitchen table and Daniel sat down before it, facing the window.

There was a long moment of silence. "I suppose you're wondering why you're here," the farmer asked, with a slight smile coming across his face. The question caught Daniel by surprise. "Leila's been having this dream that someone shows up at the door and he's been crying so much that his clothes are all wet, and it's her job to take care of him. I've learned not to take her dreams lightly. She dreamed about the fire in the rectory, and she knew the Riddle boy would fall off the bridge. So you see, you fit right in." The farmer cocked his head to one side. "Leila's a little different than most," he confided. "She teaches at the institute over in Bradford. Eastern stuff, meditation, philosophy. She can see into your past lives, and she can dowse better than anyone. Not just water, either. Out in the field, she can find tools and missing parts as if she's the one that put 'em there. So you see, you're here for a reason."

Since that evening last September when his wife left, Daniel had run into one strange event after another. In addition to the situation in which he now found himself, there was the tattered old man who appeared from nowhere at a lonely country crossroads, poked his head into the car window, and said, "There are no accidents." There had been the beautiful white goss hawk that swooped into the branches of a Douglas fir and was still there in the morning, watching him. There was the odd-looking key in the shape of a four-petal flower that he found by his mailbox and that couldn't belong to any lock he had ever seen, yet he still put it on his keychain and carried it with him. Then there was the woman in the supermarket who swore she had met him in Mexico and became angry when he insisted otherwise. Now there was this farmer and his wife who dreamed of his arrival. Daniel felt dazed.

Leila appeared at the stairwell just as the tea kettle began to whistle. "May I offer you some tea? I like green tea, but you may want some chamomile. It's very soothing." She removed some tea bags from a tin and dropped one into his cup. He was glad it was chamomile. He'd never had green tea and he wasn't in the mood to try it. He watched the steam as she poured hot water into the cup and the tea bag popped up to the surface. He started to press it down and stir it with his spoon. She sat down directly across from him, looking at him intently, stirring her own tea. The farmer sat at the end of the table, leaned his chair far back on two legs, and crossed his arms over his wide chest.

"Thank you for lending me your son's clothes," Daniel blurted out. "They seem to fit. And I appreciate your putting my things in the dryer. I sure was soaked." The woman just smiled. "Mr. Schneider tells me you're a teacher," he said.

"Karl," the farmer interrupted.

"Yes. I teach at the Institute for Eastern Studies. Have you heard of it?"

He had. In fact, someone at work had suggested he go there. "It's Buddhist, isn't it?" Daniel replied.

"It was founded by a Tibetan monk, but we embrace all religions and spiritual practices." She stopped to sip her tea. Turning to Karl, she asked, "Did you tell Dan about my dream?"

Karl nodded. "Told him you were a dowser too," he said.

Leila looked back at Daniel. "What do you think?" she asked. It was a teacher's question.

Daniel shrugged. "I suppose these things happen."

"I'm happy to hear you say that. These things *do* happen," Leila said. "And I think this dream is very special. *You* are very special, if you don't mind my saying so. You are here for a purpose." She waited to see if Daniel felt uncomfortable, but he seemed to be taking it all in. "You have been sent here to learn, and I am here to help in some way."

The afternoon sun had fallen directly behind her and all Daniel could see was her silhouette outlined in a golden glow.

He began to tell them about his life, his work, his family, and the twenty-five years of marriage that had come to an abrupt end. He told them how pained he felt that he, a Bancroft, was getting a divorce. He tried to describe his nightmares, and how lonely he felt in that large, rambling house. He described the years the family had been together, traveling out west, vacations at the beach, bringing up the children, Thanksgivings in New England, and Christmases there on the farm. He thought his whole family had been as happy as he was, but now he was learning that, not only his wife, but his children hated him for the dominating, controlling presence he had become. When had he turned into such a person? Oddly, he didn't feel ashamed to tell strangers all these things. On the contrary, he felt a sense of relief. He was hearing his story for the first time, and someone gazed back at him as witness.

By dusk, he had told them about his early career in New York, his military service, and the beginning of his days as a philosophy student in college. Leila seemed to become more and more excited as he went along. "You couldn't have come to us at a better time," she said. "Clearly, despite all that wonderful background and experience, none of it seems to be helping you now." She looked up to the ceiling, searching for words. "If I may say, there's still a huge piece of the puzzle missing. Or should I say many smaller pieces. I hope you will allow me to help you find them."

Daniel thought for a while. "I don't know what else to do."

"Every great teacher will tell you that those answers are already inside you," Leila said. "I am here to give you the tools to help you find them. It's the reason you are here. It's the reason you came upon the lamb. It's the reason you left your house today. It's the reason we have come together."

Daniel looked at Karl, whose expression said simply, "I told you so."

It was getting late. Leila retrieved his clothes from the basement and he was ready to leave.

"Will you come back?" she asked.

Daniel thought for a long moment. "I don't think I have a choice," he said.

Leila smiled. "You don't."

They made a date for the following Saturday afternoon.

It was twilight. Out on the porch, Daniel pushed his feet back into his wet socks and into his wet boots, and laced them up, cold. He shook the farmer's hand and Leila gave him a brief hug. "One more thing," she said. "You must reclaim your full name, Daniel. It brings you great strength."

Over the next two months, Daniel visited the farm practically every weekend. Karl met him as he pulled up next to the barn, then turned him over to Leila for whatever it was she felt she had to impart. At first they just talked in the kitchen, or sat on a hillside in the grass, getting to know one another. They admired wildflowers, watched cloud formations, and heard the call of mourning doves emerging from the bucolic stillness: *Whoweet,* pause, *whooo, whoo, whoo. Whoweet,* pause, *whooo, whoo, whoo.*

It was clear to Daniel that one of the first things Leila wanted to teach him about was meditation. The lessons began with them sitting on the living room floor in stocking feet, before incense and scented candles, facing one another. He had never realized what a non-stop carnival marched through his head until he learned to take time to recognize the chatter in his mind and let it move on. Then there was the breathing—the soul of meditation, she called it. In, two, three, four; out, two, three, four. Then she said, "Listen very carefully to all of your body. Learn its language. It is the single gathering place of all your knowing. Be in the Now. The past and the future exist only in your head. The Now is your doorway to everything. Timeless. Eternal." They sat down to meditate practically the moment he walked in the door, and again before he left. He couldn't have known how masterful he would become.

To gauge his progress, Leila sat before him with her eyes closed and held his hands gently in her palms, her long fingers touching his wrists. There, she could feel what was within him and guide him toward the silence. He tried to relax all the muscles in his body. "Whatever you're doing now, do more of it. You're going down." Then, as a stray anxiety rippled through him: "Now you're coming up again. Whatever you're doing, try to let that go." Little by little, he began to learn the internal language of his mind and body.

Then, one Saturday afternoon, Leila asked him, "Would you like to meet your guides?" He didn't know what she meant. "We all have guides—entities that know us and help us whenever we ask them to."

This time, she guided him in a meditation, leading him first into relaxation, and then into an ancient chapel he had never seen before. It was bare and empty and smelled of wet stone and old wood. There, she instructed him to sit in the pew at the far right front of the church. He could see, feel, and smell all the musty details as if he were truly in this conjured place. Then Leila spoke to him of his guides, who were waiting for him beyond a large wooden door that had been set into the thick stone wall along the right side of the altar. When he was ready, he would go through that door to meet them.

Leila left Daniel alone, deep in his meditation. For what seemed a long time, silence surrounded him, and gradually he was overtaken by a sense of wonder. He arose, drew the heavy wooden doors open, and walked out into a broad field of grass dotted with immense boulders and bounded by thick stands of evergreens. A mountain rose up at the far end of the field, and midway he saw his guides, huddled together. They were identically dressed in long white robes, but as he approached them, he could see that each one had a unique appearance. One of them appeared to be the leader. He had dark olive skin, a sharply trimmed beard along his jaw line, and wore gold trim along the collar line of his robe. Many had dark hair; some were blond; one had nearly snow-white hair cut close to the scalp. They didn't speak to him. They didn't speak to each other. They barely noticed he was there.

Daniel walked slowly among the guides and they made room for him to pass. Some looked him over with only gentle curiosity, then turned away. He didn't know what to make of them. Soon he tired of being among these strange entities and returned to the church. Leila's voice then took over and guided him back to the faint candle in the middle of the living room floor. She was excited to hear his experience. "Did you meet them? Were they human, or some other form?"

Daniel explained what had happened. "You mean you didn't speak to them?" she exclaimed. "They're aspects of your unconscious," she said. "You have to engage them to get them to talk back. Ask them questions. Tell them how you feel. Otherwise, they just stand there the way yours did. How many were there? Men? Women?"

"About twenty-five or twenty-six," Daniel said. "Men and women."

"Oh goodness! Most people have three or four. It takes a lot of energy to keep that many going. They must sense that you're prepared and able to hear them."

The truth was, Daniel didn't know what to think of his guides. They seemed uninterested in him, and he was uninterested in them. He didn't care how many of them there were. What he did take with him was his daily meditation, which had begun to expand his awareness geometrically. About a month later he returned to his guides in a meditation and asked them about his friend Stephen— and his life was transformed.

Between lessons, Leila disclosed insights she had about him. One day sitting on a hill, she told him, "You've had forty-three lives as a priest. You've taken thousands of vows of silence. They keep you from speaking your truth." She paused for a long moment, as if trying to grasp a vision. When she finally spoke again, she said, "You have a very old soul, Daniel, and you carry with you a great deal of pain. Your own pain, and the pain of others. But most of all, you carry the seeds of a possible conflict. You want to realize your oneness with all of creation, but to do that, you must give up your life as you know it. It will be the most challenging step you or any of us can ever take." An uncomfortable expression crossed Daniel's face. "This must not frighten you. Though there will be difficult passages, your life will change in ways you cannot imagine. Those changes may sometimes be painful, but it will be the most wonderful journey of discovery and rebirth." She paused for a moment, reflecting. "It's possible that, with so many guides, you may be headed toward the center of a very significant event. Possibly something like the Mayan prophecy. Guides tend to converge when they see opportunity for great change." She swept a strand of hair behind her ear. "Do you know about the prophecy?"

Daniel shrugged.

"Some say the Mayans were the most advanced civilization in the world. They gave us the concept of zero. But their astronomy was even more impressive. They foresaw that, on the Winter Solstice in

2012, the sun will rise in perfect alignment with the center of the Milky Way. They made that prediction over 2000 years ago. I don't think we found the true center of our galaxy until very recently. Not bad, eh?"

Daniel had never thought about the center of the galaxy, but the Mayan accomplishment seemed impressive. "Where does the prophecy come in?" he asked.

"Their calendar, which I'm told can extend back billions of years, nearly to the beginning of the universe, suddenly ends on December 21, 2012. They call it the end of the Fifth World."

"What's going to happen then?"

"Who knows? Cataclysm? Apocalypse? The strange thing is that other prophecies point to the same end date." She looked up, as if measuring the speed of the sky. "But that's all twenty years away. If you *are* meant for the prophecy, you're going to need a lot more help than I can give you. But it will all come, I can assure you. All sorts of interesting people and events will appear to show you the way. You will uncover what your heart has to reveal." She paused to gather her expanding thoughts. "The heart knows everything," she said. "Everything! When you open your heart, with the right feelings, with the right realizations, that's where you will find your truth."

Daniel received Leila's words with a mixture of dread and anticipation. As if trying to confirm her insights, he said, "I sometimes see people as children."

Leila seemed taken aback. "Tell me more."

"It happens when I am awake, driving to work, and the other night it happened in a meditation. Adults suddenly shrink to who they were as children—playing, running around. Sometimes they're happy and sometimes they're very sad. Wounded, even."

Leila's eyes widened. "That's wonderful! You're seeing them as they truly are—at a point in their lives when they begin to take on their karmic roles."

Daniel knew what karma meant, but he wasn't sure he wanted to get into it.

Leila went on, nevertheless. "Each of us is a direct extension of our parents and of their parents and back and back. We inherit our ancestors' problems—or let me say conditions—particularly our parents' conditions, and then struggle to resolve them during the course of our own lives. And we pass the unresolved portions of those conditions on to our own children for them to resolve, and on and on."

"You're saying I have some resolving to do."

Leila looked up to the sky and sighed. "Yes, but it's not what you may think. We all have free will, and the conditions we inherit are not just problems. We inherit all the wonderful things as well, such as intelligence, grace, creativity, wonder. We take on the sum of all previous human development. But it's best we don't get into that now. What's important about your visions of children is that you are having visions. You are accessing a dimension of energy that transcends linear time."

For a moment, Daniel felt proud of himself, though he didn't fully understand what he had accomplished.

"One of the ways to heal people is to heal those children you see. Yes, many of them are wounded, and almost all of them will become wounded. You can go back and heal them with love. Very often, all it takes is to hold them in your arms with compassion."

"It's interesting you mention healing," Daniel said. "The child I saw in my meditation was my friend Stephen, who may be dying of prostate cancer. I visited my guides the way you showed me, and I asked them how serious my friend's condition is. Before I knew what was happening, they said, 'We'll bring him to you, and you can heal him.' He appeared as an adult, as he is today, then he became a child running around in bib overalls, and he wanted to play. I didn't know how to play with him, but I knew he was sick as an adult and I wanted to help him. Then he became an adult again, but now he was holding his wife. The guides were all standing around and I went over and held Stephen and Julia. As I did so, a bright light came down and filled us, except it filled Julia only partway, to her waist. I kept expecting the light to flow all the way down into her, but it didn't. And then, after a while, the scene faded."

Leila waited to be sure Daniel had finished, then reached out and touched his hand. "You've just told me several extraordinary things," she said. "First, I'm glad you've engaged your guides. They showed you just a glimpse of what you can do together. Second, this is the only time I've heard you describe an experience outside of yourself since your divorce. You've gone out to help someone else besides yourself."

Daniel realized immediately the truth of what she had said. "I remember clearly that it felt as if a gust of fresh air had swept through me."

"I can imagine. For the first time in what? Nearly a year? You broke away from your own darkness. It carried you to a much larger place—to your guides and into a realm of healing. This is very powerful. Your life force was reawakened through compassion for your friend. I'm happy for you."

Leila had a way of making Daniel feel good about himself with her enthusiasm and her genuine interest in his well-being. "What's the next thing?" he wanted to know.

"The whole meditative experience with your friend. Visions come as both symbols of something else—metaphors—and as literal truths. And often as both at the same time. So it's difficult to interpret what you see. But *everything* has meaning. I don't know what to make of your friend's wife coming into the meditation, or the way the light behaved. Light is nearly always good."

Leila stood up and, with her hands in her pockets, looked out to the far hills. "There's so much to tell you. But one step at a time.

You're making amazing progress." She turned to look at him. "You have a gift, Daniel."

Three weeks later, at lunch, his friend Stephen told him, "We've just found out that Julia has ovarian cancer." Daniel reeled away from the table and stumbled into the men's room feeling sick to his stomach.

The next weekend, Leila just shook her head. "Visions carry powerful truths," she said.

"Can we heal her?" Daniel asked.

"I don't know. You can try. But that's an awful lot of pressure to put on yourself. You're so new to this." After a long pause, she said, "I think you healed your friend."

Eight months later, Julia was dead. Stephen was free of all symptoms.

At Leila's kitchen table, Daniel held his head in his hands, his eyes pressed closed.

"You can't blame yourself. You did something wonderful, too. Stephen is alive!" Leila paced. "Look. As terrible and frightening as this may seem now, what you have experienced, the gift you have awakened, is breathtaking. You are on a path you must simply get used to. It's the reason you and I have come together, and I know it will become the basis of your life going forward. You have only touched this new dimension, and its strength will grow and be with you forever."

HE AWOKE ON A BLANKET PUSHED INTO THE DARK CORNER OF
an adobe hut. It had rained during the night and heavy drops from
the tree tops still hit on the tin roof. A dog with matted brown hair
and pale blue eyes peered into the open doorway. It was morning,
possibly late morning; overcast skies occluded the time. His hip
ached from lying on the hard ground. The blanket smelled of damp
wool and dust.

The voices of women chattered somewhere beyond the hut and
the engine of a truck labored up a nearby hill. Long river grass
had been woven around his wrists and around his temples. By the
doorway stood the pair of blackened sticks he had used the night
before. He staggered around to the back of the hut to relieve himself. A trail of slug slime crossed his path. The figures of two women
receded and disappeared into the trees. He arranged himself and
moved out into the clearing in front of his hut.

Three other adobe houses lined the edge of the clearing, each
larger than his own, each surrounded by the objects of daily life:
baskets, a yoke between five gallon cans, coils of rope and wire, bur-
lap bags, an axle, piles of wood beneath bright blue tarpaulins, and
chickens pecking in every direction. Curtains hung in the open
doorways. Ribbon and dried corn stalks were posted overhead. A
brown little boy wearing only a shirt emerged through one of the
doorways and extended his hand, offering him a flower. Daniel
smiled awkwardly and turned the other way.

Now the previous night lived clearly before him, but still he felt enveloped in heaviness. In spite of the ritual cleansing, the incense, and the chanting in *Nahuatl* that were to free him of fear, this morning he felt as empty and alone as ever. Was his fright gone? He had seen the cat eyes swirling in the glasses of water, but still he couldn't tell. All he knew was that he was here to uncover what was in his heart, to find the truths he needed for the remaining levels of his journey to Quetzal. He had been promised that he would know when the time came, and the time was now.

He wandered to the far edge of the clearing and down a gradual embankment toward a stream. His body still ached, not only from the night before, but from the long trek he had made on foot from the bus stop to this remote enclave of *curanderas* and priests. The village didn't have an official name, and certainly it was not on any map, but those who knew sometimes called it *Acapec*. A woman on the bus had known when she noticed the flower key behind the netted pouch on his backpack, and she had insisted on telling him the way.

"As you leave the flat ground, follow the stream up the *cañada* into the hills," she said, "then, depending on which way the wind is blowing, when you smell smoke you will be almost there or you will have passed it." Indeed, he had smelled smoke a full hour before he arrived at the village. It was the sour smell of charcoal being baked beneath earthen mounds, a product for which the village was known.

But the village was also known as the place in which the good *brujas* had vanquished the bad *brujas*. Long ago, the place had been occupied by witches who were said to have poisoned the water of the stream and sickened or killed scores of people, even in villages far from the stream. Good witches from all the villages gathered their powers and, with secret rites, drove the bad witches away. Now, although nearly all the original good witches were long gone, the village was still populated by the caretakers of their secrets—secrets that had made it a place of spiritual healing.

Daniel knelt down by the stream and splashed water onto his face, and onto the grass woven around his head. The water was clear and frigid, but it felt good. He remembered the smoke burning into his eyes the night before; this morning they felt puffy. The water helped. To his surprise, as he looked upstream, he saw the priest Bartolomeo standing bow-legged in the water with his pants rolled up, reaching into a cloth sack slung around his neck and scattering what seemed like clouds of dust upon the surface. With a grin missing many teeth, he slowly made his way downstream toward Daniel, waving his arm again and again out over the water.

The priest had long gray hair matted against the square frame of his face, and narrow watery eyes that seemed always to be crying. Large veins protruded from the backs of his hands. He removed the sack from over his head and looked for a place to sit down. Nearby, the roots of a tall tree defined a smooth rounded enclosure and the priest motioned for Daniel to sit there with him. At first Daniel sat cross-legged facing the stream, but the priest indicated that he should turn so they faced one another. They settled into silence and, for a long while, the priest gazed with his squinted eyes into Daniel's face. Sun was breaking through the treetops above.

The priest found a small piece of red lava that had been washed down by the stream from who knows where; with it, he cut a circle into the dirt. Then, peering deep into Daniel's eyes, he placed the stone in the middle of the circle.

Daniel felt a wave of heat ripple through his body. Was the priest asking a question? Before he could think, the priest reached over and removed the long grass from around Daniel's head, gently tore the long grass away from his wrists, and then, with his eyes shut, held Daniel's hands in his own calloused palms.

Soon Daniel closed his own eyes and began to breathe slowly and deeply. He heard the gurgling of the stream and, almost immediately, his body began to relax to its rhythm. Cool air stirred over his skin, and the calls of birds enveloped him—from high above and from every corner of this far-off place. He could feel the beat of his heart and used it as a metronome to guide the pace of his breathing. He felt as if a great shell were being shed from his body, leaving him open and light, surrendered to his surroundings.

With his hands held by the priest, he felt himself floating in the stillness for a long, long time. He could feel the priest's presence—gently at first, then growing larger and warmer, until it enveloped his entire body with a level of awareness he had never known. His body swayed gently forward and back to sounds from far away. Then, from an incredible distance—piercing through all the layers that encase the world and all the sensations that coursed through his body, penetrating deep into his reverie—came *whoweet,* pause, *whooo, whoo, whoo.* His eyes snapped wide open. Then he heard it again. *Whoweet,* pause, *whooo, whoo, whoo.* And again. *Whoweet,* pause, *whooo, whoo, whoo.*

It felt like an explosion. How was it that mourning doves here sang the same song as the mourning doves back home? Thousands of miles apart! The mourning doves on the farm were connected to the mourning doves in this far-off place deep in the jungles of Mexico! They spoke the same language. They shared an essence going back perhaps millions of years. Like a shock wave, his vision spread north and south over the continents, swept out broadly over the Atlantic, over Europe, Africa, Asia, and back around. Man, animal, vegetation, mountains, oceans, the all of earth. It was all connected! He stood up and strode to the edge of the stream.

There it was! There it was! There it was! All around him. It was as if God had shaken the skies and from them fell a downpour of understanding that covered the world.

Suddenly the vision took another exponential leap: Going back and back, he saw the earth recede into star stuff, and stars as the condensing of gasses, and gasses as the first exhalation of the Big Bang from across the vast seas of space. It was all connected, from the very beginning of all creation! Of course! How could it *not* be connected!?

He was alive! He saw all things—without time, without sequence, without void—dimension upon dimension cascading in upon itself, a cosmic One. The arrival of so powerful an image plunged deep inside him to a level of knowing that transcended thinking. It was an eternal moment.

There he stood, awash in revelation that filled every corner of the universe, tasting for the first time the delicious depths of this Truth.

When at last he came back to his place on the earth, to Mexico, to *Acapec*, to the edges of the stream, he turned around and there, on the bank behind him, he saw gathered the *brujas* and *curanderas* and the priests and the children who had danced with him the night before. They smiled and giggled and moved toward him with an undulating rhythm that matched the pulse of his present being. They pressed him back toward the stream and there they began to bathe him with handfuls of water. Bartolomeo hugged him, his head barely higher than Daniel's waist. It was joyous.

That night, Daniel had a marvelous dream. He dreamed of himself as a newborn child in the full fetal position, holding only the flower the little boy had offered him, descending slowly into the amniotic fluid of the universe. He could feel its cool liquid edge rise over his skin, first touching the crown of his head, then encircling his temples, then his throat, his chest and arms, around his waist, then down his legs, closing in over the tips of his feet. Though fully submersed in liquid, he could still breathe.

Then down he went, the light from the surface above growing distant and dim, until he reached the center of the universe, lolling slowly, still in the fetal position. There, he realized that the entire

Down he went through amniotic fluid
to the center of the universe.

universe was within him—stars, gasses, nebulae, and galaxies—his form delineating its farthest boundaries. He had the profound sense that the amniotic fluid through which he descended was the consciousness of the universe, continually forming and reforming everything within it. Matter appeared and disappeared, rejoining vast dark spaces that were saturated with knowing, shaping and informing the All. There was no time, no past or future; no beginning, no end; everything simply was. Suspended in this endless state, he realized for the first time in his memory that he was not alone. On the contrary, he felt carried in the arms of all the universe. He had found the stepping stone from one life to another.

It was a profound vision.

VERY EARLY THE NEXT MORNING, SOME OF THE VILLAGERS gathered around him in the clearing. Daniel said his goodbyes, holding their small hands in his own and looking into their eyes for the last time. He wanted to remember them, deeply, possibly for a time when he would want to recapture all the details of this powerful experience. Behind him, two of the women stuffed packets of food and bottles of water into his backpack, giggling as they struggled to close the zippers. Overhead, he heard the morning contrapuntal chorus of birds, distant among them the *whoweet*, pause, *whooo, whoo, whoo* of the mourning dove. "*El huilotl*," the priest said, pointing toward the sound. "Huilotl," Daniel repeated. He hoped it would never go away.

Soon the priest indicated for Daniel to follow him down along the stream. After a while they crossed over the stream, then up a gradual incline and along a terraced field where corn had been planted. At the end of the field they came to a path worn bare by centuries of animals and travelers. Pointing toward the stream below, Bartolomeo took a stick and, with wiggly lines, drew a representation of the stream in the dirt. He then scratched a path that followed the right bank of the stream for a short distance before veering off farther to the right and winding its way like a snake to a distant point which he marked by poking the stick into the ground. "*San Sebastian*," he said. "*Mañana, dia de los locos.*" On the third curve of the snake drawn in the dirt, the priest drew a small circle, then leaned his cheek against folded hands in the sign of sleep.

When Daniel nodded that he understood, the priest reached into his pocket and pulled out a necklace of blue and yellow seeds from which hung a soft leather pouch. Then Bartolomeo showed him a small piece of red lava, the same stone he had placed at the center of the circle the day before. He put the stone into the leather pouch, then reached up and hung the necklace around Daniel's neck. Now the priest, eyes brimming with moisture, looked up into his face with the deepest compassion Daniel had ever seen. This man, this short little man, this priest on spindly legs, seemed at that moment to offer up a soul as large as the world itself, made only of love. It was such a new sensation for Daniel. He allowed his arms to enfold this paradoxical creature and held him to himself for a long, long time.

The earth in Mexico was not like the earth at home. Nothing in Mexico was like home. Here the soil was pale and had an ancient smell; the sunlight was thin and the air more brittle. Even the sound of Daniel's sandals on the gravel had a hard edge. He was so far, far from home. Clearly, his whole mind and body had gone through a great transformation and, in a strange new way, he felt that Mexico was also his home. Over and over, he felt the life force he shared with all things—with the stones he saw, with the soft sound of the air, and, step by step, with the feel of the earth beneath his feet. The awareness began to shape his motion into a rhythm; in a beautiful, rarefied way, he was becoming part of this foreign landscape.

Without warning, the voice of his guides burst open inside him. *Can we talk?*

Daniel clutched the strap of his backpack and glanced about. "Where have you guys been?" It had been days and days, nearly a week since they had spoken, and now suddenly here they were.

Waiting our turn, they said.

"A lot's happened," Daniel remarked. "There's a lot to talk about."

Yes there is.

"Bartolomeo and his people were so wonderful!"

We wonder, whatever has become of the nine-to-five working stiff we used to know?

Daniel smiled.

You're doing well. But right now, we want to go back to the stream in Acapec. We're not sure you've taken in the full meaning of this oneness you've learned about. For example, what can you do with just oneness? It's knowing without wisdom.

Knowing without wisdom? Daniel repeated the guides' words to himself. "What do you mean? It's simple. I'm part of the whole universe. I understand that. I can feel it. I get it."

Calm down. There's just more to it.

Daniel nodded surrender.

Everything is a part of the universe, the guides said. *Without understanding what that means, you may feel connected, but it doesn't serve you.*

Daniel lowered his head and tried to listen. For a long while he heard only his own breathing, then the voice came again.

There's a wonderful truth that emerges from All is One, the guides continued, *and that is that the universe will always sustain you. You are continually borne up by the very mechanism of the universe from which you were formed.*

With his head lowered, Daniel kept his steady pace along the path, trying to concentrate on the guides' voice.

The power in the universe that is responsible for all of creation is the same force flowing through you right now. Your life, your being, is a manifestation of that creative force. You must simply receive it.

"And how is that?" Daniel asked.

When you have taken your life fully into yourself, you must then surrender it all back to the universe and await its reply. Surrender and listen. Surrender and listen, over and over.

Gradually, reliving the epiphany of the day before, Daniel began to feel these words, these lessons, come into him with growing clarity. He could feel their warmth start to flow through him and he could sense the part of himself that was being carried away. Perhaps that was what it was like to listen, he thought. He savored the moment, feeling its details. Then, after a while, he said, "I'm still going to die some day."

Yes and no, his guides answered. Your body is going to die some day, but you are not your body. You are the creative force. The creative force within you will never die. It goes on, because that force can never be against itself. But the important thing now, in this life, is that you are *that creative force, alive and seeking expression.*

In a most subtle way, Daniel tasted the distant sweetness of what his guides were trying to teach him. He removed his backpack and sat down against a eucalyptus tree. Sun glinted down through the branches. What were the guides saying? It seemed so simple, and yet he knew he had captured only a small piece of it. The interconnectedness he felt was a living, dynamic force of the universe that sustained his life. But didn't it sustain all life? Wasn't it a force shared by all creation without differentiation?

The guides heard his thinking and quickly interrupted.

It's far from undifferentiated. In fact, it is your deepest essence, yours alone in the most personal way you can imagine. While you are the outcome of an infinitely complex creation that applies to everyone, the result of that creation is uniquely you.

There was a long pause, then the guides continued:

Last night you had a wonderful dream, floating in the universe. In the dream you could see that you were the universe, and that is the truth of the dream. Everything about you and the universe, going back to the dawn of creation, lives within you. It is written not only in your DNA, but throughout the all of yourself, your psychology, your unconscious, in your character, your moods, even in the aspects of ourselves as your guides. This is the truth you consult when you become still to hear your inner voice, the voice that knows everything about you, where you have been and what you are to become. It speaks to you all the time, sometimes in the most apparent ways. The important thing to realize is that your history is within you. Together, you and the universe share and create your destiny. There cannot be a more personal calling.

Daniel seemed to be in the perfect space to hear these words from his guides. They reached a place far within him, joining pieces of truths that had long wanted to be together. He took deep breaths and with each breath his understanding became more whole. It was as if a new seed had been planted and from it a much larger truth began to grow. His epiphany from the mourning doves, clothed in these fresh ideas, was transformed from an impersonal, abstract idea into a living reality that took hold of his life. He and the universe shared a destiny.

With the sun warm on his neck, he let his eyes fall closed.

6

DANIEL'S FIRST EPIPHANY HAD COME YEARS EARLIER.

Open boxes of Dunkin' Donuts had already been picked over. A few all-chocolates remained, as well as some with strawberry icing. Daniel filled a paper cup with coffee, stirred in some powdered cream and half a packet of Sweet'n Low, then looked around the meeting room for a place to sit. Morning traffic had been brutal. His neck and shoulders ached and it was only Monday. It was a relief that he could spend the morning just listening to some presenter talk about time management without having to be on his toes.

Daniel had relocated south six months earlier and, within the first week, he knew he was out of his element. He was surrounded by type A's, although he had been recruited precisely because he wasn't one of them. They thought they needed something different.

The presenter strutted with energy and enthusiasm—on a Monday morning, no less. No doubt he'd come to town the night before and arrived here this morning even before the doors had opened. His job depended on that kind of self-generated excitement, and he was here to bestow as much of it as he could on those assembled.

Suddenly, as if someone had flipped a switch, the presenter became still and deeply serious. With his head down, and without saying a word, he paced slowly back and forth. Gradually everyone became quiet.

When all the attention in the room was focused on him, he looked up and asked, "What's important?"

Either it was too early in the morning, or no one understood the question. There was only silence.

"What's important?" he asked again, looking out over the room. The silence took on a shade of embarrassment.

"Making money," someone finally said.

"Customer satisfaction."

The presenter didn't seem satisfied. "Let's try some more. What's important?"

Of course! He's here to talk about time management, Daniel thought, and just as he did so, someone else called out, "Efficiency. Optimum use of capital."

"You're a tough bunch," the presenter said with a slight smile. "Let's try again. What's important?"

The room grappled with the question. Where was this guy headed? Maybe he's looking for the soft values. "Relationships. Satisfaction. Family," someone said.

Without thinking, Daniel called out, "Survival."

The presenter turned on his heel and faced him squarely. "Now we're getting somewhere. But survival is your lowest calling. What's your *highest* calling?"

Daniel felt as if a blade had come down to lay open his life.

He was fifty-four. His vision of his life extended out no more than ten or eleven years, the age at which his father had died. There it was. His end, he felt, had been drawn without his knowing it— perhaps decades ago. Only then, in that instant, could he see it for the first time. And beyond, there stood death. His highest calling? His highest calling? Where was there room for a highest calling?

This edge, this ending, this darkness beyond had no permission. "I am my mother's child," Daniel screamed to himself. "Everyone in that family lives into their nineties. I am part of that family." Then, with a force he had never known, he strode forward and pushed death aside. Before him, in sunlight, he saw an open plane of forty more years. Another lifetime. Another chance.

Almost immediately, the vision of forty more years began to change his life. Deep inside, a profound shift took place. The presenter had exposed his emptiness and the sight of it awakened deep anguish. He remembered the ending of a poem: "What have you done with the garden that was entrusted to you?" It haunted him. What *was* his highest calling, he asked himself? He didn't know. But he knew it wasn't the work he had been doing. It took the CEO another year to notice.

Twenty-thousand years ago, shrouded in the skins of animals, a man curled up against the cold in a far corner of the cave. A fire flickered and cast moving shadows of the tribe on the stone walls of the cave. Again and again, his body remembered his utter helplessness against the great weight, the immense power of the beast—as if he had taken the beast inside himself and it had consumed him. Now he was weak and wounded, his hand missing a finger. Though he had been the voice of the gods for his tribe, the gods were leaving him and he felt utterly alone. More than pain, he felt the fear of his aloneness, like a serum that coursed hot through his veins. As his eyes dimmed into sleep, a woman came to touch his shoulder. A girl child in her arms watched him impassively. For a moment, her touch flooded through him as an awakened sweetness that carried him into his dream.

Outside, the beast growled, and terror washed over the man. The walls of the cave would never keep the beast out if it wanted to come through. The beast circled away, tantalizing, then moved near once again, a growl rumbling deep in its throat. Other voices joined it—wild shrieks and howls, some that could clearly arouse the beast's uneasy mood. Nothing could keep the beast out if it were angered. Darkness surrounded the man and the ageless smoke of seared flesh hung in the air and drifted out into the night, drifted to embrace the beast. Clearly the scent had attracted the beast. Or was it the man's life that still lingered so naked, so easy? Surely the beast had noticed. The man lay unmoving, listening, huddled in his helplessness into a small mound that might be invisible to the beast. The pain was deep, saturated by the rumble of the beast's breath inside him. Nothing could keep the beast out—nothing, not even the stone walls of the cave—if it turned its gaze and chose

*Nothing could keep the beast out—nothing,
not even the stone walls of the cave.*

to come through. It was not even a choice, but a mindless whim stirred by even the slightest breeze. The beast growled. The man ached with the beast's mood, so profoundly temporary yet final and beyond reach. After a while the presence of the beast seemed to drift away from the cave, and the space filled with the man's sickened heartbeat. His neck, his head, his chest, his arms surged with the acid of his fear. His eyes were now wide open in the blackness of the cave, as the yearning edge of hope cut through his breath. The terror etched itself again into his flesh, burning into recesses that would scar over so that he would forget. But, already, he had given part of himself to his children, a part that could not forget.

Morning came and, with it, a terrible wind that blew shards of ice across the face of the cave. The beast was gone, over the ledge, carried by the wind. The man looked out over the valley to the mountain of the gods—high, serene, and alone against the crisp morning sky, wisps of snow, like smoke, drifting from its peak. He had dreamed that, one day, the mountain would become a river of fire that would drown his people and all the animals that fed them. But the mountain spoke to them not of fire, but of abundance that would come to the valley, and of the light of the sun that would arrive to warm them.

One day, walking along the river bed, the man could move no more and he fell into its soft, muddy banks. A great white bird circled overhead. Soon floods came to cover him over and there he remained for a thousand years. When the mountain of the gods did indeed become a river of fire, it entombed everything in its path.

8

THERE HAD BEEN BLOOD IN HIS URINE THE NIGHT BEFORE. Now, at an art center far in the southern prairie, Daniel looked around and saw that he was the only guest. Various seemingly abandoned out-buildings and sheds stood in hot wind, scrub grass, and tumble weed. In the distance, massive, oddly shaped concrete forms rose from the earth for no apparent purpose. The principal exhibit began as he entered one end of a long building.

Stretched out before him, Daniel saw two rows of precisely machined rectangular aluminum-plate boxes, each identical in shape and size—72 inches x 51 inches x 41 inches, the brochure said—extending in laser alignment to the end of the room. Fifty-two sharply precise boxes, each equal to all the others, and yet structured differently internally in some subtle detail. Some had an open side, others an open end. Internal panels filled others—horizontally, or vertically, or diagonally. Some had open seams. And yet all were rigidly rectangular, solid and alike. The slight variations started to overwhelm him. "How is it possible for the next box to be different from all the ones before?" he asked himself.

Daniel left the building at the far end to enter a matching building where forty-eight more perfectly aligned aluminum rectangular boxes receded in perfect alignment, each the same, yet different from all the rest. A hundred boxes in all. The variations amid such repeated precision began to make his brain tumble.

When he left the buildings, Daniel trudged with his head down through long grass. A small snake undulated across his path. Soon, he reached yet another out-building where a replica of an abandoned Stalinist-era Russian school room had been installed. Following the minimalist perfection of the previous exhibit, the chaos of a school room from the other side of the world made him queasy. Student papers strewn on the floor, torn-open notebooks left behind, communist red, penciled notes, posters of Russian destiny unfolding, a picture of Lenin, chalked Cyrillic letters and words he couldn't understand—and outside, the whistle of prairie wind. Apart from the temperature, it could have been the Russian steppes. His head began to whirl and he went to the car to sit down. Then everything went dark.

The darkness closed around Daniel like a corridor in which excited voices caromed off the walls and ceiling. There was great rushing and yet he could neither see nor feel anything. A terrible thing had broken loose somewhere in his body and coursed through every channel of his awareness, surging. Now his body not only encompassed the corridor, but extended out to the edges of creation. Its seas crashed and flowed, then rose up again and enveloped everything in their path. This went on and on for hours—it could have been days or weeks—until time was gradually pushed aside and his field of experience was at once filled with all things and empty of all things. Finally, during a moment of silence, of stillness, of peace, the creature took one last breath and a cascade of calamities burst through every pore of Daniel's consciousness in a flood that ushered him to the tranquility of a distant shore.

"Am I dead?" he asked.

Your body is.

From high above, Daniel looked down and saw a great confusion around his body, but it was unfolding in extremely slow motion, like a cocoon of green larvae awakening gradually, striving to be born. It didn't seem to matter that he was dead. In fact, in spite of the urgency apparent below, he had never known such serenity. It seemed to reach from an unimaginable distance, to hold him in its embrace. He remembered, as a child, staring at a spot on the

"Am I dead?" Daniel asked. "Your body is," came the reply.

ceiling until it receded and receded, shaping around him an aura of resonance that extended to the edges of infinity. Now that same vastness came to hold him at its center. There was nothing, and yet there was everything—a knowing that filled him beyond, beyond reach.

You have died, but it's not yet time.

"What does that mean? Can't I stay?" Daniel asked.

We cannot be together like this for very long. You are here for transformation, not transition.

"It's so beautiful!"

I understand. But it's not yet time.

Then the knowing came toward him in the form of light, like a sunrise in the void, illuminating a path directly to his being—brighter and brighter, filled with space that invited him into itself.

"How can I stay?"

If you go, I cannot go with you. There is a horizon that will separate us.

"Who are you?"

I am you, the all of your subconscious, the all of you as an energy being.

"Are you one of the guides I met with Leila?"

I am all of your guides, and more.

"Are you my soul?"

No. I and your guides are mutable consciousness. You, in your present form, if you cross the horizon, will become eternal.

Long silences filled the space.

"It feels as if I'm in heaven."

You are at the edge of heaven.

"Are there others? I don't see anyone else."

They are in the light. They are *the light. You should be able to feel their energy, what you may call unconditional love. It's the single most transcendent experience a human can have.*

Love! That's what he was experiencing! It wasn't knowing; it was unconditional love!

What you call love is really the unifying energy of the universe. Everything responds to it. Stones, plants, mountains, and, of course, people.

"You said that if I cross the horizon you can't come with me. Does that mean I can go alone?"

You are here for a reason, but it's not what you think. You are not here to die. You are here to know there is another path. Since your awakening, you, and we along with you, have come a long way. It's much too soon to stop now. Before you there will be many paths and you are here to help choose the richest one.

"Why would you show me this incredible passage if you don't want me to go on?"

It is both a promise and an empowerment. You must know that, beyond that horizon, is the defining truth of your life—when the time comes. But for it to become so, for it to be realized in all its fullness, you must bring this experience into your life, and into the lives of others, as a tangible truth, the ultimate reality of your being, to be learned and lived and trusted.

"What you are suggesting goes against all the indescribable feelings I am having right now. I want to stay here forever. I want to go into the light. I'm not afraid."

In this very conflict you are now experiencing, you are being reborn. Struggle purifies, and there are journeys yet to be taken toward that end.

"What should I do?"

Return to you body. Heal. Then prepare for a journey to the ledge of Quetzal in Mexico.

"Where is that?"

Trust that one of your guides will show you.

Before him, there appeared flashes of jungles, bones, hooded priests, and a snow-capped mountain. "What will happen to me?" Daniel asked.

Do you remember how you feel when you look up at the heavens? How you have yearned all your life to be at one with all the universe? Quetzal, and your journey to him, will help you fulfill that yearning.

"But I already feel that oneness, right now."

Quetzal will open before you a path even richer than the one you are on. If you take it, you will not wish to cross the horizon until your work is done.

There was a long silence.

We love you. God loves you. Trust us. You cannot fail.

The voice paused.

It's time to go back.

9

DANIEL HAD HIKED INTO THE NOONDAY SUN AND INTO A
wooded area when he caught what he thought was the faint
smell of charcoal drifting up from the village he had left behind.
But this scent now carried a sweetness that had not greeted him
earlier as he followed the river upstream toward *Acapec.* Then he
realized it wasn't the making of charcoal at all. It was incense, burning *copal,* something he had smelled all through the cleansing ritual.
Somewhere in these woods, another ceremony was taking place.

The scent of *copal* grew heavier as he walked on. Soon, ahead
of him, he saw a shawled figure move through a shaft of sunlight
and then disappear. Dry sticks cracked under his feet and he suddenly felt as if he were invading a private space—not only with his
body, but with his sound. He stopped and the silence of the woods
expanded out and away from him, into the air that threaded itself
deep into the trees. His heart pounded in his ears. As he looked for
a path that would lead him around the ceremonial dome of presence
that filled the space before him, the small shawled figure stepped
out from the shadows and onto the trail in front of him. She looked
directly at him and with open palms invited him toward her.

Daniel recognized her as one of the old women who had knelt
beside him during the cleansing ceremony. Silver bangs fell from
beneath the shawl over her head and a black blouse with large
pink flowers came down her arms. The texture of her skin was
like scalded hot chocolate. Keeping her eyes fixed on Daniel, she

retreated a few steps and gestured toward an altar that had been built off to one side of the path. There, an urn of incense smoked among burning candles. Behind it, on a mound of earth, stood a statue of the Virgin of Guadalupe. Fronds of herbs lay in a shallow bowl of water and, to one side, a clay mug boiled over a small fire.

The woman helped remove Daniel's backpack and invited him to sit before the altar. She gazed at him for a long while, then turned to stir the steaming mug and removed it from the flame. Sun filled the clearing. Soft air brushed around the fire and carried the essence of *copal* into the trees.

The woman removed the clutch of wet herbs from the bowl and shook them over the fire, then poured some of the water into the mug. She presented the mug to Daniel and indicated that he should drink. *"La abuela,"* she said, with a knowing nod and a crooked smile. It was a warm dark-brown liquid that smelled sour and swept Daniel with a memory of rotting leaves in the fall. Surely if he drank it there would be no turning back. He looked down into the mug, then up through the trees and into the blue Mexican sky. The woman touched the top of his head and smiled down at him. He choked down half of the warm vile juice and the bitter grounds suspended in it, and handed the mug back to the woman. His tongue and the inside of his mouth felt coated with tingling grains of sediment.

From a red-and-yellow woven sack that hung from the stub of a broken branch, the woman removed a knife, a lime, and a small plastic bag of red and brown petals. She cut the lime open, crushed some of the petals in her hand, and squeezed drops of lime juice onto them. With her thumb, she mulled the mixture into her palm until it turned bright orange, then painted the concoction on the center of Daniel's forehead. Without warning, she scooped up hot ashes from the fire and branded them into the same spot. *"Aci teonantli,"* she said in *Nahuatl:* May the Divine Mother arrive.

Daniel felt as if a hole had been burned open between his eyes. He sat enveloped in the smell of lime and smoke, as the woman massaged his temples. In an instant the pain was washed away and in its place the living spot on his brow grew to fill the entire crown of his head with a warm, pulsing energy. Then the woman offered him the statue of Guadalupe to cradle in his lap and, with her ring finger, delineated the band that arched over the Virgin's belly. *"En cinta,"* she said. Daniel had seen a hundred images of Guadalupe, but never before had he noticed the Empire sash. A wave of dizziness surged up through him. The Virgin of Mexico—perhaps the Virgin of all the Americas—was pregnant!

It was difficult for Daniel to know how much time elapsed—minutes, perhaps hours—before visions of unimaginable origins began to overtake him. Nor could he know how long the visions lasted. Looking down, he noticed that the Virgin had become a luxuriant pale-blue scarf draped in his hands, and his hands, his fingers, were those of a woman with long, smooth nails. His wrists were cuffed with beautiful gold and silver bracelets, but inside the jewelry were sharp teeth that bit into him.

Nor was his skin pink and ruddy, but now the color of cinnamon. He saw his legs folded under the scarf—smooth, young, and barefoot. Now he could feel his whole body—lips, arms, breasts, hips, the recesses of womanhood—and the rise and fall of his breathing. Where there had been hardness and strength, now there was the softness of flowing water. But the water was delicate. It felt as if the very air passed through him.

What had been curls of eucalyptus bark scattered on the ground became mottled phalluses that drifted up under the scarf and into his being. He leapt up with a scream and, though he saw nothing, he felt hands crawling all over his body. Again he screamed and danced to shake them away, but there was nothing. A man dressed in armor passed on a horse without noticing him. Nevertheless, Daniel hid and covered himself until the horseman was gone.

Suddenly the leaves and pine needles that hid him fell to the ground and began to undulate beneath him as if lifted on a bed of air. He reached out and clung to a sapling to steady himself. But he had no strength in his hands and arms, and the churning earth flung him to the ground. He landed on his back with his legs and arms spread wide, looking up through denuded trees to a pink-and-gray sky. Rising into his body from the depths of the earth were the sounds of engines and of children crying. Overhead, black clouds raced like smoke before the wind. Carried on the wind, he heard the words, "Silence the bitch, silence the bitch, silence the bitch."

Terror swept through him as if unseen armies were about to crest the hill. Instead, what he saw emerge from the trees was an old woman—blind, and clutching with two hands a bowed crutch that replaced her missing leg. She had a worn sack slung over her shoulder; from it hung the heads of calla lilies. As she hobbled forward, her pale, milky blue eyes rolled up toward the sky. She tucked the crutch under her shoulder and, with her free hand, touched his face. Her hand smelled of soil mixed with the oils of plant leaves; it felt rough on his skin.

Then, as if she could see, she touched the center of his forehead and a great sun burst before his eyes. But it was not the sun. It was an immense fireball that scorched the land and seared the flesh of hundreds of bodies leaving them strewn on hillsides and in ditches, some clinging to one another. A vast empty silence expanded out from the scene like waves of concussion, leaving only flames and soundless black smoke. He felt himself scream, but heard nothing. Soon, he realized he was cradling one of the corpses in his arms, rocking back and forth, filled with love. It was someone he had known, but he didn't know who. Its face was desiccated and distorted in pain. The body weighed nothing, like a brittle corn husk. There was no time. Purple and red light filled the sky.

Minutes passed—perhaps days or years—and the terrain was swept smooth by the wind.

*As the blind woman hobbled forward, her
milky blue eyes rolled up toward the sky.*

Scars in the earth healed over and filled in with long grass and crocuses, as if born from the will to wholeness that surged through him. He could feel this wholeness stretch out over the land. Where there had been corpses, there were now piles of clothing neatly folded and boots to hold them down against the wind. His consciousness drifted among these markers as if to touch people he had once deeply loved. A great sorrow rose up within him, sorrow couched in an even greater compassion. He began to howl, and now the power of his compassion filled the hillsides. He felt as if his heart would burst.

Through his tears he saw a band of women arise from the hillsides—watery, ghostly images coming toward him—and from afar they howled with him. They came, surrounded him, lifted him to his knees, stroked his body, and smoothed his hair. From among them a tall middle-aged woman emerged, her hair pulled back, the skin on her face taut. She had the appearance of an older Guadalupe. The woman reached out, held his hand, and looked deep into his eyes. Then a great pain shot through his belly and, from beneath him, she removed a newborn child. A baby girl. The woman offered him the child, now wrapped in the blue scarf. "Witness the power of the Divine Feminine," she said, "mother of the new consciousness." Then the women stroked him some more, touched the child, and lifted him to his feet.

When at last he opened his eyes, the old woman was standing before the altar. She received the statue of Guadalupe from his hands. *"Teonantli,"* she said. He saw that his wrists were red and punctured, as if from small teeth. He couldn't see the smudged spot on his forehead.

As he continued his walk through the woods, he was suddenly startled from within.

Quite a trip, his guides said, laughing among themselves.

"Did you see that?" Daniel exclaimed. "My God!"

Your God, indeed!

"What was that all about?"

Even we don't know. But we can imagine. It's a realization you may want to keep in mind when you meet Quetzal. It may have to do with what's going to happen later on.

"But what does it mean?"

That's right, you don't know Nahuatl. Teonantli. It means you've just experienced the divine feminine, friend, and our guess is that our days as lone and willful men are numbered. The party's over.

IO

THE NEXT MORNING, BY THE TIME LIGHT BEGAN TO FILL THE far edge of the valley, Daniel had descended the other side of the ridge, catching glimpses through the trees of beautiful distant mountains bathed in early sun. By now, he had crossed a broad piece of the valley. He began to hear what he hoped were the church bells of San Sebastian from somewhere up in the distant hills, along with the pop of sky rockets. His heart grew with excitement. As far as he had come, inside, he still felt a deep yearning for completeness.

Part way up the hill, where his path joined a dirt road, he saw a cart with large wooden wheels, drawn by an ox adorned in lace. In the back of the wagon were a half-dozen raucous celebrants wielding obsidian axes, their green-and-red-painted faces peering out through the jaws of jaguar heads, their bodies draped in jaguar skins. They cheered at the sight of the white man and invited him aboard. He handed them his backpack and they helped him up while the cart kept moving.

Sacks of human hearts made of papier-mâché were moved aside to make room for him in the cart. One of the jaguars offered him an orange. They laughed and shouted and patted him on the back, and he didn't understand a word they were saying. Then, with the sharp edge of a tin plate embedded in the cart floor, they cut holes for eyes and mouth into an empty cotton sack and pulled it over his head. It smelled musty and slightly sweet. Enclosed in the pale white light, he heard great laughter all around him. He had become one of them as the cart bumped toward the town.

Barrages of rockets surrounded in a glare of fire whistled up into the sky and a band thumped with a beat that reverberated through the streets. The concussive force of explosions pressed down upon them. The cart pushed through a thickening crowd and finally came to a stop. The smell of gunpowder and smoldering paper hung in the air. As the jaguars jumped from the back of the cart and over the sides, Daniel was carried, hooded, into the throng along with them. He could barely see out the small holes of the sack, yet in front of him he made out the folded green spikes of a bobbing jester's cap. He felt his body being pushed from side to side as they pressed their way through a narrow street, moving gradually toward the center square of San Sebastian.

There seemed to be music everywhere. Coronets, clarinets, drums, and trombones made every manner of dissonant noise, held together by the steady *boop* pause *boop* of the tuba and the sound of smoke-filled explosions overhead. Several times he felt something strike his head and then realized that paraders were throwing candy to onlookers who lined the streets, some hanging from windows, some peering down from rooftops. Streamers of square tissue paper of every color spanned the street like a canopy. A dog on one of the rooftops was going wild and seemed likely to fall off each time he lunged forward to bark. Someone to his right held a live iguana on his shoulder, while ahead, a flatbed truck with its own sound system carried a caged beast that danced and recoiled before a real fire.

When the procession reached the square, it followed a cobblestoned street around the periphery. On walkways through the center, men on stilts strode beside gypsy midgets. A bonded pair in black and white represented light and shadow, except the shadow led the light. *Mojigangas*—body puppets twice the size of a man—in images of an exiled president, a mother-in-law, and a prostitute cuddling a lascivious priest to her bosom, bobbed through the crowd. At the far end stood the cathedral, its bells ringing.

On a bandstand in the middle of the square stood elegant death—the classic *Catrina,* a skull with hollow eyes peering out from the shade of a large plumed hat—dressed in a black satin bustle, a feathered boa draped around her neck, a folded parasol hooked over her arm, and, in her skeleton fingers, a long cigarette holder.

Daniel moved with the crowd to the rhythm of a band as sky rockets burned through the air and exploded overhead. He was pushed along one side of the square, then down a narrow street festooned with more colored tissue paper. More candy flew through the air. Someone threw an arm over his shoulder and his heart suddenly seized. He threw off the sack from his head and reached behind himself. He had forgotten his backpack! His heart raced. A flash of heat rushed over him, followed by profuse cold sweat. He charged through bodies to reach the edge of the crowd and began to push himself through the oncoming procession back toward the square. He stepped on feet and elbowed mothers with children, fighting his way through a tight sea of onlookers and freaks and incessant noise. Suddenly, pain shot up from his shin as he tripped on the pedal of a bicycle and fell forward into dresses and pants and dark skin in shoes that stepped aside to make room for him. When he looked up, two *mojigangas* loomed twelve feet above him, as if to demand, "What are you doing here?"

Someone helped him up and, for the first time, he felt ashamed to be so clumsy, so out of place among these people who seemed to make no judgment of his difference. But he had to find his backpack—in it his passport, his money, the keys to his house and to his car at the airport. If indeed that backpack was to be found!

As he threaded his way back to the square, he berated himself for being so stupid. "This is Mexico!" he exclaimed to himself. "They steal everything!" When he reached the square, he dashed through the central promenade, dodging iron benches and fountains and men on stilts, until he came to the narrow street from which he had entered. It was still thick with bodies moving toward him.

The mojigangas *loomed twelve feet above
him as if to demand, "What are you doing here?"*

He turned back up along the side of the square to another street that
entered from the north. It was practically empty. He ran one block,
two blocks, three blocks, past stores and parked cars, then turned
left. Where was the cart? Where did it drop us off? He thought he
was only one block east of the street they had come in on, the length
of the square, but the street he came to was empty. There was no
tissue paper canopy. He turned right and saw *La Catrina* coming
toward him, the boa slung over her arm. He ran past her and up the
empty street. Then, out of the corner of his eye, he saw the deco-
rated ox and the cart in the middle of a narrow alley, facing him. His
backpack hung from the right horn of the ox. Zippers and Velcro
hissed as he checked each pocket and pouch. Everything was there.

By afternoon, the procession had disbanded and Daniel sat beneath
the shade of a large tree that overhung an entire corner of the square.

Families who had come to see the *locos* now relaxed with their children. Carts with ice cream and fruit waited for customers and great clouds of balloons swayed in the air. As he gazed about, he realized that the incredible noise that had filled the square was gone. Now, just the church bell rang on a schedule known only to the faithful.

But now, more than the sound of the bell came from the church. Now, carried on the air, he heard the chanting voice of a priest and the soft, murmured response of congregants. It drew from within him feelings of gratitude. He entered the church, stepping over the thick wooden threshold, worn smooth through layer upon layer of grain, and saw a stone font with holy water. He was not a Catholic, but nevertheless he dipped his hand in the water and crossed himself as he had seen others do. The smell of incense and candles hovered with the cool, resonant sounds of high-vaulted ceilings. Saints in glass cases lined both sides of the nave, each fronted with a tiered array of flickering candles. The wall behind the altar bore intricately carved solid gold and images of angels and cherubs that surrounded a life-size Christ, crucified and bleeding.

Daniel didn't feel he was one of the congregation, now on their knees, and so he drifted toward several small altars along the left side of the church. Toward the front was a small chapel tucked in beside the main altar. Through the short, stone doorway, he could see a warm coral-pink light shining on the other side. The room seemed to glow. He peered inside and saw five rows of empty pews. He slid into the middle pew and gazed up toward another life-size image of the thorn-crowned and crucified Christ, eyes cast up to the heavens. Here, the sounds from the main area of the church were muffled, but still suggested feelings of surrender. The warm coral color that filled the room comforted him. He had so much to be grateful for. He removed the small piece of lava from the pouch that hung around his neck and held it gently in his fingertips. Then he closed his eyes and began to meditate.

There was no face, only a pearly light.

As he descended deeper and deeper into sublime consciousness, he felt his body begin to rock gently forward and back. Vague images of light and shadow danced through his awareness, as his consciousness expanded outward and outward. On his left, he had a remote sensation that someone had moved into the pew and sat down beside him. He struggled to remain centered, but the energy of this new presence pulled him up from his depths, and a sweetness filled the air. Glancing down through half-closed eyes, he saw that the person next to him had cracked and swollen fingers, caked with dirt. The hands, one holding a gardenia, emerged from dark brown sleeves. Raising his eyes, Daniel saw a figure in a hooded robe seated beside him.

You have given your life away, and we are here to take it back.

Daniel heard the voice resonate in his head, but it didn't seem to come through his ears. It was a voice much larger than the size or the demeanor of the figure seated next to him. But it had no resonance within the walls of the chapel. It was a sound that arose from deep inside him.

You are hearing my thoughts, the figure said. The words seemed filled with compassion and yet held an edge of urgency and impatience. *I don't have long to be here with you, and there is a great deal to tell you.*

Daniel leaned forward to look into the shrouded face and saw only a pearly light that arose from somewhere within the robe and filled the hood. There was no face. There was no head. Just an empty robe with ancient hands coming out of the sleeves.

You left your life in the care of an ox. As he said this, the figure opened his right hand; in it was the flower key. Surprised, Daniel quickly scoured through the pockets of his backpack and found nothing. Indeed, the key was gone and, somehow, this man, this being, this robe of energy had found it. Instead of giving the key back to Daniel, the figure closed its dirt-encrusted hand around it.

Your life has an embedded destiny, the figure said. *Are you prepared to hear me? You must not let that go.*

Daniel turned to look directly at this engaging figure, intent to listen.

Think of all the circumstances of your birth, the figure went on, *none of which you had anything to do with. You are a singularity, you*

and each of the six billion of you on this planet. Each of you is the heir
to a unique, immutable starting point.

The words reverberated in Daniel's head. Embedded destiny.

Today, you and your people are afraid to think of yourselves as the
center of the universe. But long ago, you were the center of the universe.
The sun and the moon revolved around you, the stars and heavens
around them. Today, instead of being at the core of the universe, you
have become a mere speck among specks in the outermost reaches of
an unimportant cluster, one among billions upon billions of galaxies,
embracing exponential numbers of stars, your sun among them—dim,
average, indescribably irrelevant. But in spite of endless cosmic redun-
dancy, the insignificance of your galaxy, your solar system, your planet,
your teeming continents—each of you is absolutely unique!

For a moment the figure became silent, as if searching his
thoughts. Daniel strained to grasp the scope and significance of
what he was hearing.

In the course of this unintended diminishment, something very im-
portant has been lost: your point of view. You have discounted the
single most evident and differentiating aspect of your experience: the
fact that your life is born into and carried out in the body you have—
the eyes you see through, the hands you use, your mind, your heart. No
other creature of the billions upon billions that fill this world has been
brought to live within the body you now occupy, the singular living
being which only you can call "Me!"

Daniel could feel his passion rising.

Your experience is utterly inexchangeable: the air you breathe, the
sounds you hear, the feelings and thoughts that course through you.
Only your eyes cry, only your heart aches or swells, only your voice
speaks the words you feel and think. Only you behold the power of
the sea, the majesty of a distant storm, and the mystery of a crescent
moon. Only your ears hear the thunder of a waterfall, the call of birds,
and the soar of a Beethoven symphony. Only you feel the ache from
weariness, the sorrow of lost love, the dearness of being held.

As the figure said this, his hands came up over his heart, as if remembering a time when he had felt the sorrow of lost love, the dearness of being held.

What's more, the figure continued, *you are perfect. From the dawn of creation, all the forces of the universe were set into motion, and every detail from that instant on has been an unbroken chain of events culminating in the totality of Now. Nothing has failed. It's a perfect system. It can't be otherwise. By its nature, the process has defined itself through its unfolding and made manifest all of creation. Everything, from the energy at the farthest edges of the universe to the cells in your finger, have been born of that perfect system—the sum of all cosmic events—and they are themselves perfect. Like the perfect gardenia I hold in my hand— the bursting out of its petals, its creamy velvet color, its intoxicating perfume, its rich green leaves, the rigidity of its stem, even the browning edges of its petals and its eventual death. It's a perfect system born of a perfect system. You, like the gardenia, have been born of that system as well, and you, too, are perfect. You can't be otherwise.*

For the first time, Daniel felt his heart open to receive the fullness of the Present and his perfection in it.

By whatever route you have come, the figure said, raising his arms to the heavens, *the principle that wrought creation is still your seed. Its voice, its consciousness unfolding, is the very life force that breathes within you. Moreover, you bear the imprint of every occurrence, every turning point—from the primal spark, out across an unbroken plane of events, sometimes through the narrowest of passages that have led to your present being. Memories born at the dawn of consciousness, transformed among stars, coupled and re-coupled, have been carried over the stepping stones of great distances, every link and permutation fused into the rich and unimaginably complex essence of your being, pressed into the awareness of your cells, each coded with the singularity that is you. You are the voice of all that has come to you.*

The figure fell silent, its hood bowed forward. Daniel heard his heart beat in the stillness.

Beyond the self you have given away lies the vast realm of your larger self, the plane of profound understanding that shimmers before you, silent and unexplored. In moments of clarity you can feel its presence, the unspoken knowing of your unrealized wholeness. You may experience it as a wisdom that flows to you from the farthest edges of the unknown, and draws you to itself like a mother's arms, asking you to look into its eyes. But the vision is overwhelming and you turn away.

The hood seemed to shake with the passion.

You should take a bite from your own flesh and hold it under your tongue to remind you of the taste of your truth, never to abandon yourself again.

You are now past the noon of your life. It is time to know once again your larger self. Know that your life is precious and immense beyond measure. The whole of your self, with its eons of wisdom in concert, has been speaking to you from the moment you were born. Your life is not a benign path laid out before you, but a manifestation of the universe itself. Your life is nothing less than the burning point of consciousness unfolding. There isn't a mission or a destiny more important than the life you are living. Stand firmly on its highest ground. Open your arms wide, feel the wind before you, breathe in its freshness, see the distances beyond distances of possibilities. You are not apart from anything. You are the center of everything. The reality of Now, the truth of what is to be, is yours to create. Breathe into it, and it will itself breathe into being. You are the crucible of creation. Live it!

The voice stopped. Daniel had listened from within, feeling the figure move and speak. His heart felt full and floating. He had never heard such words. For a long while, he sat without moving. The glow of the chapel seemed to shimmer around him. Candles at the altar danced within small halos of light, and he felt a rush of heat surge through his arms and up into his neck. He realized he had been crying. His eyes burned and felt puffy. Tears had dried on his cheeks. The figure next to him remained still, its hood bowed slightly forward.

"Do you hear what I am feeling?" Daniel asked.

I feel the all of you.

Daniel gazed down at the padded kneeler in front of his feet, at his hands folded in his lap.

These truths I have given you may be too great for you to embrace all at once, the voice said, *as may be the truths that came to you through others. But their underlying power has been revealed. When you sit with Quetzal, these truths will be ignited within you. They will come alive and you will be transformed.*

The figure paused, and Daniel thought he detected a smile on the face that was not there.

Then you will truly *wonder what to do with your life.*

Silence fell between them. A bell tolled high above. Then the ancient, swollen hands of the figure reached over and placed the flower key into the pouch that hung from Daniel's neck. By opening his hand, he asked Daniel for the small red stone he still held and Daniel placed it in his palm.

You must give this to Quetzal, he said. *It is you, born at the center of the universe.*

Then he added the stone to the leather pouch and folded it closed. A soft, opalescent light shone from the shroud. Then he handed Daniel the gardenia and its scent rose up between them.

"Who are you?" Daniel asked. The entity only patted the back of Daniel's hand.

Tomorrow Quetzal. Go south and then west up into the mountain. Follow the ridge, keep the valley to your right, and listen for the call of the chachalaca. It's a shriek that makes men tremble. Tonight you can sleep up there, he said, pointing upward. *There is a small space under the belfry where they keep the ropes. May you have a restful night. Tomorrow you will climb all day.*

With that, the shrouded figure slid out of the pew and drifted through the small stone doorway and out of sight.

Daniel sat in silence for a long, long while, then bowed his head and lowered himself to his knees. On the surface, his body felt fluid and smooth, like the water of a serene lake. And yet, deep inside, far into the center, it felt like waves crashing upon the rocks. The hooded figure had revealed to him the wonderful next steps on his journey to wholeness and, at the same time, had awakened a deepening dread of the price he would be asked to pay when he reached Quetzal. He prayed for resolution.

When his feelings had ebbed into surrender, he went out into the square to watch the people, find some food for that night and the following day, and bathe himself in the early colors of an evening sky. Looking down, he saw that he still held the gardenia. He held it up to his nose, then tucked it safely away in his backpack.

That night, it took hours for sleep to engulf him. The events of the day were simply too overwhelming. He could still feel the sack over his head with its rough-cut eyeholes and its bittersweet smell; he could still hear the concussion of sky rockets. And then there was the hooded voice and the message he had come all this way to hear—a dimension of knowing that lifted veils he never knew were there. He had stepped into the unreal and it made his mind tumble. He tried to make sense of it all, and there was no sense to be made. These were the conditions that Mexico forcibly evoked—a living contradiction of history and mythology, religion and pain—a contradiction that, in the end, would pitch him into a realm of utter surrender to the truth of its reality, and the truth of his own.

When sleep came, it took him to a time of great darkness.

II

He would never forget the feeling. The CEO called him into his office, looked into his eyes, and said, "Dan, this isn't working out." As he looked back at his boss and realized what was happening, fear tore through him like fire. In an instant, his primal self bubbled to the surface. It felt as if he were going to explode. He had never lost a job in his life. He had a huge mortgage, car payments, insurance, credit card debt, a family to support, a house to maintain, practically nothing in the savings account, and he was fifty-five years old.

These were the hard facts of his vulnerability. Daniel kept them in a tidy bundle in the back of his mind, and always knew they were there. In an instant, that tidy bundle burst open, and his entire body seized up. His ears began to ring. He saw the CEO speaking to him, but the words were drowned out by the onrush of fear. He protested that it was the wrong thing for the company to do, that the role he was playing was critical and not yet finished. When the soundless dialogue ended, Daniel arose, like a wounded soldier who lifts himself up to march on, and with all his strength and bearing, strode resolutely past familiar faces in the hall to his office.

Vulnerability is an invitation to annihilation. To show indecision, to reveal even a glimpse of the tumult that lived inside him would have been to be cut from the pack and eaten alive. And, oh, he'd seen others eaten! The beast senses opportunity and would set upon him in an instant. The beast was always there—in the halls, on the shop floor, behind the desk, in the glass office, on the street at night, across the dinner table—watching. To expose himself would be to identify himself as the next to be eliminated. It was the law.

It seemed to Daniel that he had to distance himself from the truth of himself, whatever that truth might be. He must scare away the beast—trick it, feign power he didn't have. And so, on that morning, Daniel tried to bury the utter terror that was building inside him. By the time he reached his office, his whole body was shaking. "How can my arms be strong enough, my heart large enough, to overcome the onslaught of this endless foe?" he asked himself. "I'm going to die."

That night, and each night for weeks to come, Daniel awakened abruptly in the early dawn, seized by fear. It embraced him with its hot breath, made his heart pound, and bathed him in a layer of cold sweat. Night after night, the dark intruder arrived, announced by the distant howl of an approaching train.

Gradually, over many nights, Daniel began to separate himself from his fear. It became something apart from him, a wave that crashed over him if he lay still. Then one night when it arrived, to his surprise, Daniel said, "Oh, it's you again!" He had the presence to step away from the fear, to let it pass over him and through him without allowing it to cling. Several nights later, he did the same thing and, this time, as fear washed over him, he invited it to stay. They stood before one another, motionless. His fear seemed to breathe— a large black shadow the size of a car spilling off the end of the bed. Slowly, Daniel began to move around it.

These were the edges of his unconscious. The fear was real, but not real. He knew it arose from deep inside. If he could just think clearly enough, he could retreat from it and watch. It had substance, and yet it was just a dark ephemeral energy. As Daniel beheld his fear, he could find no rational explanations for it. It asked for all of him—it confronted him with a darkness he could never fill.

That night, and on other nights, Daniel and his fear came more and more into balance. Eventually, it shrank to the size of a pillow.

Before long, the dance, the gentle gazing at one another, became intoxicating. What he thought were overwhelming realities in his life became virtually unimportant. It didn't matter that he had no job, that his savings would last only two more months, that huge bills were coming in, that he was too old to be rehired, that it was a tight job market, or that he had no prospects in sight. Daniel had surrendered himself to a much larger truth and, in doing so, was able to stand face to face with fear, embraced by serenity. He felt only acceptance and a quiet sense that he was being reshaped to fill a larger purpose. Everything would be all right.

12

It rained during the night. Long before dawn, Daniel was awakened by roosters crowing and an acolyte stepping over him on his way up to the belfry. Now the bells began to toll, first one and then the other. The sound reverberated down into his small alcove, waves of dissonant vibrations that he could feel on his skin.

Daniel put on his sandals and the acolyte led him down the ladder with a flashlight. Votive candles glowed before the saints and cast a dim, rose-colored light out onto the pews. Soft incense filled the air. The acolyte showed him into a small sacristy that also served as a bathroom.

The water was cold, but felt good on his arms and face. For the first time in weeks, he saw himself in a mirror. His beard had grown—a dark brown with patches of gray along the chin. Always clean-cut and trim-suited, he hadn't worn a beard since college. Now he was a different person. His skin had aged and his blue eyes, once alert but shallow, now held a deep softness. He approved of what he was becoming. In fact, he had longed for it—longed for a time when he could shed himself and be reborn to a larger purpose.

As he left the church, the bells were ringing once again as people came in for early mass—dark-skinned farming men in stained white clothing with red sashes, holding their straw hats penitently before them; women, some carrying children, wearing slightly more colorful skirts and blouses, but shrouded beneath dark shawls that covered their heads and shoulders. The people crossed themselves and bowed with bent knees as they entered.

Puddles of water glinted in the square and two dogs hunted for food beneath a park bench. In this quiet morning air, no one could have imagined the *locos* chaos that had engulfed everything the day before.

As Daniel reached the far end of the square, he heard a faint, brittle voice calling from behind, *"Peregrino! Peregrino!"* He turned to see an old man carrying a long stick rocking toward him. Daniel turned back to meet him.

"Buenos dias," the old man said, bowing slightly and catching his breath. *"Usted va al templo de Quetzal?"*

Daniel nodded. *"Si, en la montaña,"* he said, gesturing toward the south.

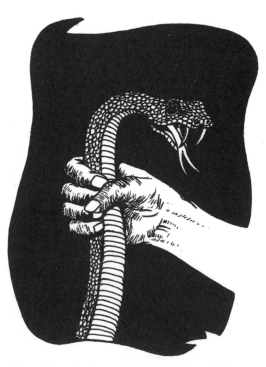

*Daniel took the staff. What he couldn't see
was the entity that lived within.*

"*Esto es para usted,*" the man said, and handed Daniel the stick. It was a beautifully polished staff of grained dark wood with a gnarled head that tapered to a chambered tip bound in brass. Then he noticed that it was much more than a polished stick. It was a gracefully undulating serpent with intricately carved feathers instead of scales. The gnarled head, cocked upward to form a curve, included fangs, a forked tongue, and green eyes that gleamed like emeralds. Daniel ran his hand over the entire length of the staff, admiring how the layers of feathers had been carved to match the grain of the wood. It seemed to be a magnificently crafted work. What he couldn't see was the entity that lived within.

"*Para mí?*" Daniel asked, placing the tail of the snake on the ground.

"*Sí, sí, un regalo para usted,*" the man said, but seemed disturbed by the way Daniel handled the staff. He took it from Daniel's hands and inverted it so that the curved neck and head of the snake rested on the ground and the tail pointed upward, then he handed it back. To Daniel, it didn't seem at all right that the head should be pointed downward. In fact, it made him feel extremely uncomfortable, but he didn't argue. Nor did he allow the head to touch the ground.

"*Y esto es para el templo,*" the old man warbled, removing from beneath his jacket a thick cylindrical candle, on the side of which was an image of the Virgin of Guadalupe. "*Si me hace el favor,*" he said. "*Para el templo.*" Then he reached into his jacket pocket and offered Daniel some small cakes wrapped in green tissue paper. "*Para comer,*" he said, gesturing toward his mouth.

Daniel understood and laid the candle and the cakes carefully inside his backpack. Then, once again, he ran his hand over the staff he had been given and nodded to the old man. "*Muchas, muchas gracias,*" he said. "*Muy, muy bonito.*"

"*Que Dios lo bendiga,*" the old man said, bowing slightly and cocking his hand toward his head in a gesture that was part salute, part blessing, and part goodbye.

Daniel, about to leave, turned to address the old man. *"Como se llama?"* he asked.

"Penitente. Penitente Diosdado, para servirle," the old man said.

"Yo me llamo Daniel Bancroft," he said, trying to affect a Spanish pronunciation, and they nodded their heads toward one another, smiling.

"Que Dios lo acompañe," the old man said, and Daniel waved goodbye.

When the old man had faded back into the darkness, Daniel turned the staff back over and dug the brass tip into the earth.

With the faintest glow of morning coming into the sky, Daniel followed a cobblestoned street south out of the town, past small houses tucked into the hillside. A man on horseback trotted toward him going the other way. Soon the street turned to dirt and the solitude that grew around him became complete. With his eyes to the ground in order not to stumble on large rocks that lay about, he began to develop a pace suited to the terrain. He knew the climb would become much more arduous as he made his way up the mountain—above the clouds, they said.

After a while, all vestiges of the town disappeared behind him and he fell into a rhythm of walking and breathing, his eyes cast only a short distance ahead. He could see the path disappear into the trees ahead and he poked the earth in front of him with his new staff, feeling its rigidity. He had never used a staff, or a walking stick for that matter, but it was a gift, a beautiful gift, and he would learn to walk with it. It added an extra beat to the cadence of his stride and made a solid sound when it dug into the earth.

"You should take a bite from your own flesh and hold it under your tongue to remind you of the taste of your truth, never to abandon yourself again."

The words came rushing back like a rogue wave from the sea. The encrusted hands, the otherworldly glow from within the hood, the sound of the voice filled all the space within him.

"Your life has an embedded destiny. You must not let that go."

It was as if the words had been burned into his consciousness.

"Each of you is absolutely unique."

"What's more, you are perfect."

The voice swelled and carried him from within.

"There isn't a mission or a destiny more important than the life you are living."

"You are the crucible of creation."

So many thoughts and feelings now rushed toward him. They filled his emptiness. This was what his heart had yearned for whenever he looked up into the night sky—to be one with the universe. Now he felt more and more embraced each day. But at this moment, the most important realization seemed to be that he had given his life away and he was here to take it back.

He remembered the feeling he had when the hooded figure described living through the focused totality of his being, ". . . the eyes you see through, the hands you use, your mind, your heart . . . only you . . . only you."

It felt as if his body were indeed the center of the universe.

He filled his lungs with morning air and felt a surge of freshness course through his body. It was all in the Here and Now. Within this body. Embracing consciousness. The focal point of all experience. In the growing light, he took time to observe the details that surrounded him—the sounds of birds, the stones beneath his feet, the bark on trees that had been scarred deep brown by the rubbing of cattle and the beaks of birds.

"The whole of your self with its eons of wisdom in concert, has been speaking to you from the moment you were born."

Wasn't that what the guides had told him just few days before—that the universe speaks from within? I have only to listen, he thought. "I am listening. I am listening," he called aloud.

The feeling of oneness that had overtaken him with Bartolomeo came upon him once again, this time laden with reverence, gratitude, and awe. Or was it like the unconditional love he had felt when he died? That was beyond recapture, but it was all from the same source. Belonging. Whole.

As he entered the foothills, the path now lined with ferns and tall grass, he noticed sudden movement out of the corner of his eye. There, part way into the grass, was a graceful thin snake about the length of his forearm. Without thinking, he picked it up and, as he gazed into its round eyes, the body of the snake relaxed into his hands. He stroked it gently along its entire length, then allowed it to crawl into his shirt and around his waist. It seemed the most natural thing in the world to do. He and the snake felt as if they were one. Indeed, at that moment, he and all the universe were one. The snake snuggled up against his warm skin and didn't move.

The air felt cool and moist. First light now filled the sky like a soft veil. Somewhere off to his right, Daniel heard the gentle gurgle of water running off the mountain. Trees started to thicken around him and held a voice of their own, close and flowed through with air. He breathed it all in.

Today, he would reach the ledge and meet Quetzal. The thought rushed over him like a sudden gust of wind over still water, in a swirl of both wonder and dread. The scope of what he was about to do seemed overwhelming. Here, alone on a mountaintop, he would gather up a lifetime and—what? Ignite it? Distill it into a cup of goodness? Throw it away? And by what means? Lightning? Evaporation? The incandescent touch of the divine? Death? How is an ordinary life transformed? What does it even mean to be transformed, to realize your divinity?

The mystery and anxiety that had been seeded in him as far back as his exchanges with Leila now awakened and grew like a bittersweet vine throughout his body. What would he be asked to surrender? Parts of him had tasted the eternal, and it beckoned with greater sweetness than ever before. He remembered the day he died. There could be no greater lightness and knowing. It made him hold his life with an unexpected gentleness—hesitant, tentative, precious. His life could slip though his fingers in an instant and that would be alright. It's what looms ahead that kept his anxiety burning. Quetzal.

Without warning, he burst into a catharsis of laughter and tears. The mountain enveloped him with both sadness and love, and his cries of joy and sorrow carried out through the trees and into the space beyond. It was as if a great weight had been removed. His heart felt open and free. Head down, he trudged on.

Not far along, through the trees, he noticed a small pyramid of stones mounded up waist high in the center of a smooth clearing. A bundle of twigs lay between two circles of ashes. It occurred to him that this was an altar of preparation to be used before reaching the ledge.

Removing his backpack, he crossed his legs and sat before the altar. Breathing deeply, he closed his eyes and allowed stillness to overtake him.

This is a powerful mountain, his guides said. *We all feel your release.*

Still carried on the waves of his recent experience, Daniel listened. It was often the case that his guides felt as he did and, early on, he had wondered if indeed he was feeling what the guides felt instead of the other way around. He learned later that he and his guides were all different aspects of the same person. And weren't his experiences the experiences of all the universe? The thought expanded within him. It was true, but sometimes too fragile for him to grasp.

Come be with us.

Now, deep into his meditation, he felt the hardness of the ground dissolve beneath him as he descended first to the stone chapel that was now so familiar to him, then out the side door and into the green and shaded clearing where his guides awaited him. He walked among them and they touched him on his arms as he passed. Their leader, Melchior, taller than the rest, stood toward the rear.

Daniel knew that in their presence he must speak first, so he began, "Why are we here?"

To prepare your mind and heart for Quetzal, came their united voice.

A short figure with dark skin and black hair pushed his way through the other guides and looked up into Daniel's eyes.

I am as frightened as you are, he said. It was Carlos, a guide who had spoken with rapture of his baptism in a river at the hands of a Spanish priest nearly 500 years ago. *We will be before Quetzalcoatl,* he said. *Remember, I have seen Quetzalcoatl and it's not a small thing.*

Melchior came forward and put his hand on Carlos's shoulder.

You saw Quetzalcoatl, a god of the past, he said. *We will be before Quetzal, a god of today. There is no comparison, other than that they are both gods of worlds in transition.*

That's frightening enough, Carlos responded.

Melchior seemed disturbed. Looking out over the others, he asked, *Aren't we all here with Daniel to be reborn ourselves? To transcend this insanity that has grown up around us? Do we now shrink from the journey?*

Rhetorical questions all. Again and again, the guides and Daniel had reviewed the scope and purpose of their journey together. From the very first, they had described a panorama of transformation that was nearly incomprehensible. They would guide Daniel along his darkest passages and through all the years ahead, including all the challenges of this final and culminating journey.

In the beginning, it had seemed not only daunting, but impossible. As Leila had predicted, their main interest was the Mayan prophecy, then twenty years out—a prophecy that the world would come to some sort of harmonic convergence on December 21, 2012. Others who knew of the prophecy spoke of catastrophe and Armageddon, of legions being carried off to distant realms of the universe, the end of the world as we know it. And Daniel was supposed to prepare for this event! At that time, Daniel barely had enough foresight to see his way to work and back, yet these strange beings, these guides that Leila had brought him to, described in detail the journey of trial and transformation that lay before him.

The guides tried to prepare him for every passage, but he didn't trust who they were, and this sometimes led to tension between them.

Don't think we can't leave you, they said. But they never did.

Still, weren't they just figments of his imagination? Even Leila had said they were aspects of his unconscious, and what is that if not the imagination? How could he believe them? The thought that gave pause, however, was that they got every detail right. The job losses, the epiphanies, the vacant wandering. Even the day he died they had predicted that something profound would happen. All along, however, their passion for the Mayan prophecy, for themselves and for the role Daniel was to play, eclipsed all other considerations, and so this journey into Mexico had come to be.

I know some of you joined us mid-way, Melchior went on, *but most of us knew before Daniel was born that there would be no turning back.*

Still, Daniel doubted. He was an ordinary man, brought to this juncture by what so easily could be perceived as a series of accidents. Destiny? Purpose? He had difficulty applying these words to himself. "You know my heart," he said to his guides.

We do, and we don't accept your doubt. Your remote visitations have amply demonstrated not only your gift, but the hard reality of timeless interconnectedness—divinity itself—and everyone's ability to realize themselves as part of it. You can no longer turn away from it.

They never allowed him to forget the meditation with his friend Stephen and his wife, Julia. Over and over, they pointed to that event as evidence of his role, not only to heal, but to realize his divinity, for himself and for all people.

You have touched the other side, they said. *What greater proof do you need?*

At first, it seemed like a parlor game—to visit sick friends, only to have them get well through the ministrations of modern medicine.

You visited them as children and held them with love, the guides reminded him. *You healed the child. Of course they would get better.*

Then, one day not long ago, in a meditation, he came upon a man he barely knew who refused to see a doctor and would surely die. He found this man in the white light of dying, and spoke to him. The man kept floating backward then forward, his whole body awash in blinding light, and, like Daniel years ago, the man wanted to stay. Suddenly Daniel saw the man as a small boy crying before a vast field of flames, his face smeared with ashes. "I've burned the mill," the boy said. "My father will never forgive me."

Daniel went up to the boy and put his arm around him as the man he knew who was dying. "Is your father alive?" he asked.

"Yes," came the reply.

"Then you must come back to receive his forgiveness."

Several months later, Daniel met the man at a party. He seemed strong and healthy.

"You saved my life," the man said. Daniel held his breath. "This may sound strange, but when I was dying, you came to me and spoke to me about my father. You said he would forgive me if I didn't die. Two weeks ago he forgave me and then died in my arms. He was ninety-seven."

Daniel was speechless. He had never had such spoken confirmation. And with that, the guides surrounded him. Melchior himself was angry.

In the many years since you have had your gift, you have never trusted it. You have treated it like some sort of trick, when in fact it is your essence, he said. *It's as real and important as anything that will come to you. Maybe now you will not squander your strength.* He shook his head.

Now the guides surrounded him with their bodies.

We're in this together, one of them said.

Trust, said another.

Your insight has never been greater, said Melchior, looking him squarely in the eyes. *Go, and let it serve you before Quetzal.*

Daniel felt as if the guides had also touched him as a child and as a man. He left a branch as an offering before the altar and renewed his climb.

As he made his ascent, higher and higher, the trail eventually narrowed. The path clung to the side of the mountain; its edge fell sharply away to his right. In places, the stone of the mountain had been cut away to create steeply ascending footholds, and he wondered fleetingly how he would keep his footing on the way back. The staff no longer served him in this terrain, so he had strapped it to the side of his backpack, and now he could feel its length and awkwardness tugging behind him. At times, when the passage was only the width of his body, he clung to the mountain and to tufts of vegetation that grew from the stone. He couldn't look down.

The snake, curled around his waist, sensed his fear and, at intervals, stiffened against his flesh for a moment. Unconsciously, Daniel stroked the snake through his shirt. With each step, loose gravel skidded out into the empty space below. How he wished for his hiking boots instead of these flimsy sandals with tire tread for soles. But he was glad to have his down jacket to protect him against the growing wind and cold. At these altitudes, he could feel his heart beating and, from time to time, he stopped to catch his breath where the trail widened out to a ledge. But his rests were brief, because the sun had started to lower in the sky and he had no idea how much farther he had to go.

The call of the *chachalaca* had guided him since noon, and indeed, even from far off, it was as terrifying as the hooded figure had described—a thick cackle, then a scream, followed by a long howl as if from a dying man. Though the sound was now much closer than before, it seemed to recede farther and farther ahead of him, carried on the cool wind that flowed through the trees and around the mountain. He continued to climb, moving higher and higher up the slope.

Loose gravel skidded out into the empty space below.

Gradually, the trail emerged above the tree line, and the sky opened up; he could see far out over the valley to the north. It was filled with golden afternoon sun, splashed with dark hills and thick green forests, bordered in the east by sharp stone cliffs thrust up from the valley floor. Ahead, the trail climbed still higher, following the contour of the mountain to the left and out of sight. Daniel paused to breathe in the endless panorama. Far in the distance, a large bird banked white in the sun.

Moving slowly back to the trail, eyes fixed on the loose gravel now beneath him, he continued the climb. Once, without thinking, he looked over the edge and his body seized up. "I'm afraid," he said aloud.

You will be safe, the guides responded.

He had gone only a short distance further when the path cut abruptly around a great rock outcropping. There, revealed before him, exploding against the sun, was an immense volcano capped with snow, so close it seemed he could touch it. It was the very same cone-shaped mountain he had seen when he died! Now the sun shone pink on snow that oozed like thick icing down the steep slopes. It was all he could do to press firmly back against the outcropping to keep from being drawn over the edge, into empty space, toward this overwhelming presence. More than an unimaginably beautiful discovery—the air, the sky, the snow-covered mountain before him, even the stone citadel on which he climbed—the whole panorama suddenly seemed to hold an energy that he could feel all over the surface of his body.

Beneath his shirt, the snake felt the effect as well and began to rise up along his chest to poke its head out from his collar. He felt the snake probing under his chin and tried to stroke it back to calmness, but it slid out over his shoulder and coiled itself around the staff that protruded above his backpack, its head snug against the carved head and gleaming green eyes on the staff.

Daniel wondered, can this be the ledge of Quetzal? Had he arrived? His heart started to pound. I must be close, he thought.

Then, as if in response to his question, the chilling call of the *chachalaca* came to him from somewhere high on the top of this mountain where there were no trees for birds to roost. The scream carried out over the valley and toward the sun. Stepping carefully along the sharp edge beyond which there seemed to be no end, flush with this new energy that warmed him against the cold wind, Daniel moved along the trail. He had gone not a hundred paces when an immense, wide stone ledge opened before him. To his left he saw the large opening of a cave. He stepped onto the ledge— level, solid, and safe.

Immediately, the tension that had built up imperceptibly in his body began to drain away. Through the cold, he could feel the warmth of the sun, now almost at eye level, shining directly on him. Embraced within this warm energy, which shimmered through his body, he took a deep breath, and then another, and then another. With each exhalation, the muscles in his neck and shoulders released their grip and, for the first time in days, perhaps for the first time on his entire journey, he felt that he belonged. As far from home as he had come, as foreign, bewildering, and exotic as all his surroundings were, this was where he was meant to be. He felt as if he had been here long ago, almost as if he had been born here, and he had never known anything like it.

The sun, soon to set, shone directly into the cave, illuminating the back wall and casting a thin reflected light into a chamber that receded on his left as he entered. He peered into the dimness and felt the cool smell of damp stone and dust enter his nostrils. Midway along the front wall, previous pilgrims had built an altar that held the red waxed-paper remains of votive candles. Behind them, he saw charred branches and the cores of pine cones that hadn't finished burning. He realized then that he hadn't brought wood for a fire, thinking he would be among trees and would be able to find some. Those scraps of kindling that might have served him tonight were far back on the trail, an impossible trek in the declining light. He remembered the bundle of twigs he had passed by the pyramid early that morning; he had thought it was an offering. Now he wondered if it had been left there for him.

He would have to make do with what socks and shirts he had for warmth and what shelter the cave provided against the wind. To take the chill out of the air before going to sleep, he could make a small fire from the unburned sticks that lay in the bed of ashes. If it became too cold, he could even burn his staff, although he sensed that would be a sacrilege. Now he looked around and wondered where and how the god Quetzal would appear.

Daniel removed his backpack, carefully extracting the staff from the loops that held it in place. The small brown snake was still coiled around the head. He stroked the snake gently; soon it relaxed, then it draped itself over the staff and fell a short way to the ground. As he propped the staff against the wall of the cave next to his backpack, he saw to his right, above the used votive candles, a large outline of the flower key etched into the stone. Filled with faint traces of red and soot, it was the exact image he carried. He recoiled, as if pushed by a force radiating from the wall. His heart leapt. He pulled the key from his pouch and the two shapes coincided perfectly. What did this mean! What did the flower represent? How could this happen!

Daniel felt as if, in an instant, his entire life had been shifted into another dimension. It seemed as if time and experience had collapsed and he suddenly felt the distant edge of overwhelming fear and pain. What was happening? These two flower images, thousands of miles apart, how could they come to be? And even more mystifying, what brought them together? For a long while, he gazed back and forth at the two images. Then, as if to discharge the feelings that coursed through him, he held the key in one hand and touched the image on the stone wall with the other. In that instant, he was filled with peace and a choking desire to weep. As he tried to catch his breath, Daniel realized there could not be a stronger validation of his journey.

When at last he returned the key to the pouch, he moved to the entrance of the cave to watch the sunset. The sky had turned orange, lavender, and purple, and was laced with long undulating clouds of pink and gray and gold that gathered around the pyramid of snow on the mountain before him. Its peak still caught the setting sun and seemed close enough to touch. Soon, only a fine strip of crimson defined the far edges of the valley below and Venus gleamed like a dot of silver above the horizon. Higher still, a thin crescent moon hung like a cradle against a dark velvet sky.

After a while, he shoved his fists into the pockets of his jacket and went back into the cave. Now the walls exhaled a cold breath that carried faint traces of ancient smoke and the sound of emptiness, which receded into the blackness of the cave that had no end. Daniel removed the thick Guadalupe candle from his backpack and, on the altar beneath the symbol of the flower key, lit the offering that had been entrusted to him. The light created a small dome of comfort that encompassed the image of the flower on the wall. There, within, he ate two of the cakes the old man had given him and took a few sips of water. The flame of the candle danced before his eyes and the image of the Divine Mother, red and cream and green, took on a comforting warm, translucent glow.

Before long, his eyes grew heavy. He gathered up the charred remains from earlier fires and, using the red waxed paper as starter, managed to rekindle the sticks and pine cones into a satisfying flame. Gradually, he fed larger sticks into the flames until the fire took hold. When it seemed he had created all the warmth that was possible from these meager resources, he braced himself within his jacket and curled up on the floor of the cave, using the folded hood of the jacket as a pillow. Outside, the wind had died down and a close stillness filled the cave and the canopy of firelight that hung over him. In spite of the cold, he felt safe. The fire burned on with the same warmth and intensity long after he had fallen asleep and none of the charred branches or pine cones were consumed.

During the night, when the sun was in exact opposition on the other side of the world, the staff, propped up against the wall, fell forward and the head of the snake with its burning green eyes fell into the fire. Soon, the resins within the wood hissed and began to smoke; after a while, the entire head suddenly burst into flames. The green eyes grew larger and the head began to expand and turn black. The head grew larger and thicker and longer, and the flames that flared around it turned iridescent green and blue and gold and pink. The head stretched up from the flames and drew more of the staff into the fire. Now Daniel awoke to find the black head of a snake with a body as thick as a man's waist, enveloped in flames the colors of burning copper, bobbing over a circle of fire.

Forgive me if I am silent, came the meek voice of Carlos from deep within.

The eyes of the snake gazed back at Daniel like green fire; the snake's double tongue darted. From deep within, Daniel felt as if his body was still asleep, a cavernous drum from which a profound whisper, entwined in its own breath, reverberated, *Don't be afraid.* The blackened snake drew more and more of itself through the fire, twisting its growing body out across the floor of the cave, until it was the length of five men. It glowed in burning colors, the tip of its tail transformed into shimmering gold.

The deep whispered words still resounded through Daniel's body. *Don't be afraid. Don't be afraid.*

They washed through his heart, down his arms and legs, up into his throat, behind his eyes, and into the crown of his head,

The great snake arose flaming from the fire.

bathing his entire body in a profound sense of peace and joy. The overwhelming vision before him, far from being frightening, was a magnificent presence of sublime power and beauty.

I come before you as I come before all men, in the form to which their hearts are most open: as thunder, as wind, as a blind man begging, as light, as angels, as children in song, but you see me as I am most beautiful to behold.

With that, the creature folded itself back and moved out onto the ledge. Daniel followed. There, it extended itself along the entire front edge of the stone, like a barrier of fire between Daniel and the infinite emptiness that lay beyond.

After a long while, the voice whispered, *You have brought me a gift?*

Daniel quickly fumbled through the pouch around his neck and withdrew first the flower key and then the small piece of red pumice. He offered the snake the lava.

The snake studied the piece of stone; its gaze followed up Daniel's arm to behold his face. *With that stone, draw a large red circle in the middle of the ledge and place the stone at the center.*

Daniel did as he was asked.

You have given me the gift of yourself, and I honor you in return as the center of the cosmos. Then, gazing at the key, the snake asked, *You have seen the image on the wall?*

Still filled with the wonder of its discovery, Daniel exclaimed, "Yes! But I don't know what the flower means, or how it got there."

It's not a flower, said Quetzal. *It's the hand of a four fingered man.*

Daniel was dumbfounded.

Long ago, a man with only four fingers drew the outline of his hand on the wall of the cave. Hundreds of pilgrims have come to see it, and the image has been made into a talisman. But yours is special.

"How is that so?"

Do you remember how the image came to you?

"I found it ten years ago under my mailbox in the United States."

And how do you suppose it got there?

"I have no idea. I had stopped thinking about it until this afternoon when I saw it on the wall of the cave. I kept it for good luck."

It was carried to you by a great white bird. You see, all the cosmos encourages your destiny, even that long ago. The whisper paused, as if taking the measure of the man, then said, *Tell me how you felt when you saw the image on the wall.*

"At first, I felt fear and pain, but it was not mine. It seemed to belong to another dimension. Then, when I touched the image on the wall, all that fear and pain drained away, and I felt good, but sad."

Quetzal seemed pleased. *We must rest until the sun rises,* he said. The colored flames along the snake's body began to dim and Daniel's body grew heavy. Feeling exhausted, he returned to his fire, which now burned with all the colors of Quetzal. He promptly fell asleep and into a dream.

In his dream, he heard the wailing of a woman carried on the smoke of war—gray and metallic to the taste. Villages, burned to the ground, smoldered without a soul in sight. Shattered pottery, crumbling adobe, and barbed wire littered the way. The land lay bare, dead, the air saturated in sorrow. His own body heaved. "What have we done? What have we done?"

He wandered from hut to hut looking for some form of life, but there was only emptiness and the sound of the wailing woman.

He ascended into the sky and, from high overhead, saw in the distance a long bright object moving slowly through a cloud of dust toward the horizon. As he drew nearer, he beheld that it was a great silver-and-gold scorpion encrusted with jewels, its tail cocked forward as if to strike itself. It moved slowly and heavily, rocking from side to side. Beneath the scorpion, he noticed countless small legs. He swooped down to look underneath the silver-and-gold shell and there, bearing the full weight of the creature, were 100,000 people from all the nations of the world . . .

men, women, children . . .

. . . hollow . . .

. . . driven by suffering to the very edges of their lives.

When Daniel awoke, the fire had gone out and faint colors of rose reflected back into the cave. He stood up slowly, profoundly drained by the power of his dream. From the mouth of the cave, he saw the god Quetzal at the far end of the ledge, his thick body coiled around its own tail in a pyramid the height of a man's chest. The snake gazed at the snow-covered mountain, whose pointed peak, high above thick clouds, now captured the first light of dawn. The flames that had enveloped the snake during the night now lay flat along his entire length, like annealed metallic feathers of iridescent green and blue and gold, and pink like the folds of snow on the mountain. It was as if the two entities—in color, shape, and majesty—had in some way been born of each other.

Daniel walked up to Quetzal and nearly laid his hand on him. "I've just had a very disturbing dream," he said.

The serpent turned its head toward him. *It's a dream all men carry in one form or another.* The whispered words resonated within him with the same depth and dimension as before.

"What does it mean? The scorpion? The thousands and thousands of people suffering?"

The scorpion represents the promise of transcendence. The dream brings together the world as it is today and the human yearning for the world as it could be. It's a dream of transformation for all people, and it's the reason you are here.

"It felt like a dream of the horrors of mankind. War, poverty, inequality, starvation."

You must let that go and not judge. The snake's head moved from side to side. *Two of the most important feelings to carry in your heart are compassion and understanding. Mankind is barely emerging from the shadows of its primal beginnings. If you are to transcend that darkness, you must be forgiving of its origin. You, too, have brutalized your fellow man. But you must forgive yourself.*

The remark penetrated deep into Daniel's feelings.

A time of great change is coming. As the gate opens to that change, you must be prepared with a much larger vision of yourself and of all mankind. If you are not ready, you will pass through the gate without notice and continue in darkness.

"Is the larger vision you refer to our divinity?"

The snake cocked its head slightly, as if in pleasant surprise. *Yes.*

"Is the gateway of great change what is foretold in the Mayan prophecy? The date of alignment on December 21, 2012?"

Exactly.

Daniel lowered his head and was silent for a long while. "I thought I had thirty more years. I didn't know I was here for the prophecy. That's only a few years away, and then, if you believe it, the world could end."

The world as you know it is *going to end. It's ending already. There will be a great shift in consciousness, as if everything were turned upside down. Even right now, you are standing above a great rift along which the earth could shift and new volcanoes could erupt clear across this latitude to the heart of where the Mayan prophecy was born. But the Mayan prophecy is an opportunity, not a curse,* the snake exclaimed. *It defines for all mankind a time of cosmic alignment in which you can transcend primal darkness into divinity, not a time of doom. Awareness among only several hundred thousand of you is all that is necessary to shift the direction of world consciousness when it transects the confluence of events on that specific date. If not enough people have been awakened by that time to create the shift, the world will simply continue on the dark course is it following now. It would be a shame to miss this opportunity, but it could happen. If the shift does occur, then there will be a great change in consciousness in the years and centuries ahead. Either way, you do have thirty more years, and there will still be much to do. More than you can imagine.*

"How does realizing our divinity fit into this?"

The snake raised its head and, for a long while, gazed out at the snow-covered volcano. Then at last it spoke in a penetrating whisper.

When I incarnated as Kukulkan and gave the insights to the Mayan people, the jewel of my message to them was that, by the end of the Fifth World age, 2012, they and all creatures could transcend duality and realize their divinity. They could become one with the universe. God. But they couldn't understand this. For them, divinity could only belong to the gods. I promised them that if they entered their hearts they would be made whole and would realize their divinity. It was a truth they much needed.

But the priests in those times were profoundly taken by their belief in a polarized cosmos—male and female, dark and light, good and evil, the sun and the moon, God and man. In contrast, divinity is unity with the cosmos. The all encompassing feminine. Oneness with all that is. Duality is merely a lesser form within the larger truth of wholeness. The Mayans were not prepared to receive such a truth. Here they had seen into the very womb of the galaxy, but they failed to see their one-ness with it—that they, too, were born from that center. They even argued among themselves over the meaning of the alignment and what would come to pass. And so the promise of divinity was never written down. It was lost for all these centuries—until now, as I speak to you.

The snake looked directly into Daniel's eyes, as if to probe his understanding.

By clinging to duality, my people continued their need for war, sacrifice, and bloodshed. Your world is repeating the same mistake today. Separateness.

Daniel felt bewildered, as if he, too, would fail. "I can see how our separateness has led us to where we are today."

The snake allowed its eyes to fall closed, as if in gratitude. *I sense that you can see this. Good! It is an essential first step.*

"How else could we bring such atrocities on our fellow man? How else could we violate the earth, calling every bit of it our own? Even our greed, which has created such a chasm of injustice between rich and poor. It's all through separateness."

Through the falsehood *of separateness,* the snake corrected him, looking off into the distance.

It's ironic, the snake said. *Like many civilizations, the Mayans were looking to anchor their beliefs to a central truth, a point of cosmic stillness. But the earth and the heavens are in constant change. Their cycles never truly repeat themselves. After centuries of searching, they thought they had found stillness at the center of the great serpent in the sky, the Milky Way. It was a far-reaching realization. They aligned their temples and cities around this belief. Their sacrifices and rituals were attempts to harness what they perceived as the one cosmic constant.*

But the Milky Way churns with the same great motion as the rest of the cosmos. Had they received the divinity I offered them, they would have recognized that the cosmic center they were looking for was within themselves.

The snake seemed to shake its head in some sorrow.

Your divinity is the largest and most powerful truth of your being. It is totally transcendent of all things. And once the truth is realized, it becomes a moral imperative that can change the world.

The snake paused.

So you see, the promise must be retold.

Daniel didn't know how to respond. He had no idea there was such a grand plan in the works, and it seemed daunting. He wanted to lead a spiritual life—to be left alone to enjoy the details of love, caring, friendships, and beauty. Most of all, he yearned to bathe himself in his growing relationship with the universe, learning to trust, to surrender, and to sit with his emerging image of God. The yearning to be whole with the universe that he had felt for so many years was barely beginning to manifest, and now this.

"I am one of the several hundred thousand?" he asked.

I hope so.

"How are they chosen?"

Everyone is chosen. Only some of them hear the call. Mostly, they are middle-aged people who have experienced awakening pain, as you did. Some are young, and some are even children with old souls. They are people who "get it," as you might say, and they make their realization their life's work. They will be like seeds of transformation scattered over all the world. You probably know some of them already. When you are aware, you recognize one another right away.

Indeed, Daniel thought of several people whom he might now recognize as kindred souls, one of them being Leila. "Is Bartolomeo one who has heard the call?"

Yes. And now he is a Caller.

"Am I to become a Caller?"

I can't be certain. I would like you to be the one to retell the promise. That's why you are here, to be empowered by your oneness with Source. You become a Caller when you make the realization of divinity your life's work. There will come a time when you will see three lights streak across the night sky. If you have become a Caller, you will know they point you in a direction toward which you must return. Once you have taken the first step onto this path, much as you did when you were asked "What's important?" there is no turning back. But you have yet to realize your divinity, and that step is entirely up to you.

The choice the serpent offered stirred a dread that Daniel had felt more and more acutely since his journey into Mexico had begun.

"What does that mean?" he asked. "I already realize my divinity.

I have had visions of my divinity and the divinity of others. I have seen my connectedness to all things and to God."

That is true. But your visions only open you to receive your oneness with divinity. You have not yet stepped into your visions to assume fully the power offered you.

The voice paused, as if to allow him to receive the challenge of what had just been spoken.

There is a Plane of Divinity that underlies all things, it went on. *When you step onto that plane, you assimilate the pure cosmic truth that forever sustains your being. The dimensions of your life expand exponentially, then and there.*

As the rising sun cleared the ridge above the cave and its first rays struck the bright metallic scales along the serpent's coiled body, the creature began to undulate from within, as if to receive the warmth. The colors gleamed in the light—green, blue, and pink.

You have come all this way in search of wholeness, the snake said. *Tell me, how do you think you got here? What do you think you have learned?*

"How far back do you want me to go?" Daniel asked, searching for a place to start.

Where do you think the beginning lies?

Daniel thought for a while. "My divorce," he said. "I had never known such pain until that moment. I had never felt so lost."

You had set yourself up for that, Quetzal said, with a slightly impatient tone in his whisper. *As a young man, you, in particular, had a yearning to be held by the heavens. But then you emptied yourself of reverence and awe, in favor of reason. Weren't you told that you had lived forty-three lives as a priest? You put all that aside to embrace reason. There was no longer room for mystery and a larger relationship with the cosmos. So when the divorce came, you had nothing to fall back on. The same thing happened when you lost your first job, and in the desert when your heartbeat started to leave you. You still held on to your old beliefs.*

"I thought reason was a pretty good starting point from which to find the truth. I still do."

It is! But like words themselves, reason alone can't transcend the final barriers of paradox that surround ultimate truths. You need your heart and mind together. This is a very important lesson. Truths can only be realized from within ourselves and from inside the truths themselves. We live inside the truths and the truths live within us. Just as God lives within his own creation while, at the same time, he is his own creation. You come to your truths with both thought and feeling, using the whole of your awareness. You see that the larger truths, such as God and your divinity, are immutable. But what happened after the divorce?

"After the divorce, mystery started coming back into my life almost immediately. Look at Leila Schneider. Where did she come from?"

You suspended judgment and allowed her to manifest. You knew you didn't have all the answers, and you permitted new solutions to come to you. It's the best thing you can do, not only in a crisis, but all the time.

"Well then, I guess suspending judgment was one of the first things I learned. It has allowed me to come to this place and to be with you without fear, to receive your guidance."

Are you quite certain you have suspended all judgment?

Daniel thought for a moment. "I'm sure I haven't."

It's a curious thing, judgment. You couldn't suspend your judgment when Penitente tried to point the tail of the staff toward the sky. That meant you were not fully prepared to receive new ways.

"I still can't understand that request."

It symbolizes that I came to the earth head first, with my tail pointing to the cosmic center from whence I came. But interestingly, precisely because you could not invert your staff, I was born to you head first, which is as it should be.

The head of the great snake looked out toward the snow-capped mountain, then turned back to Daniel.

Are you without fear?

Daniel reflected for a moment, and ceded the serpent's insight.

"I'm afraid of what may happen up here. I don't know what you're going to ask of me. But I do feel peace in your presence."

I am glad. But didn't you overcome fear? Those nights after you lost your job?

"Yes. The night I invited fear to stay. I'll never forget it."

I remember it, too. It was wonderful! You didn't try to run away from fear or deny its presence. Instead, you accepted it as a part of yourself, but a part that can't harm you. In fact, you embraced it without touching it.

"It was a huge shadow that would have consumed me had I touched it."

Fear is a necessary vestige of your primal heritage. It can be beautiful, a stepping stone of transformation. Detaching from it as you did is one of the most important steps you can take toward realizing your divinity. That same detachment must serve you now. Don't be afraid.

Daniel remembered the dark nights after losing his job and he could still feel the ecstasy that awaited him on the other side of fear. He wanted to experience that ecstasy again. Then he remembered the greatest feeling of them all.

"The most profound experience I had was when I died. I was truly cradled in the arms of heaven. If only everyone could know what awaits them on the other side."

There is a reason that came to pass. Long, long ago, your heart was torn from you. Your heart failure was a shadow of that memory. But now the experience will carry you through the darkest times.

"It felt like pure love. And I didn't even go into the light. What is it that lies beyond the horizon the voice described?"

Beyond the horizon, you become that love, which is all-knowing divinity.

"I certainly didn't want to come back."

Are you glad you did?

For a long moment, Daniel was silent. "I don't know," he said, shaking his head slightly.

Do you remember what the voice said to you?

Daniel searched his recollection, wondering what the serpent was looking for.

You were told that your experience was both a promise and an empowerment. That when your work is done, a path will open before you even richer than the one you sensed when you stood at the edge of the light.

Daniel remembered.

This ledge you stand on, the sun and wind that envelop you, that volcano ahead rising up through the clouds, here and now. This is the beginning of your work.

Daniel, of course, knew this. He had known it from the moment his life had expanded out before him that morning during the time-management seminar. He had been given forty more years—and this high ledge, this immense and beautiful god-serpent, and that snow-covered mountain that towered above all things was the reason. But that didn't diminish the anxiety that had come alive the instant he had seen the great mountain in yesterday's sun. Though he felt peaceful and safe in the presence of Quetzal, he knew there was still a part of his journey that remained unfinished.

As the sun filled the front of the ledge, the god Quetzal slowly began to uncoil himself. His great head moved down the side of his body, green eyes gleaming, tongue darting. As if gliding on a bed of air, he reached the far end of the ledge and his body, shining with all the furnace-burned colors of the night before, stretched full length, resplendent in the sun.

What else do you remember?

"The power of the question, 'What's important?' I remember asking it of myself over and over for years. Even today. It's like shining a beacon that cuts through the meaningless clutter that spills into my life. It helps me regularly clear away the unimportant to make room for what *is* important. I can honestly say that it was the power of that question that led me here. Every time I asked it of myself, my guides rose up and showed me the way. Step by step, they opened the path for me to rejoin myself. Nothing else has been more important. And so I am here."

Indeed.

Daniel walked to the edge of the great flat stone and saw that thick clouds like cotton still hid the land below. It seemed that the snow-covered peak of the volcano before him had grown even higher, and now towered above the clouds flooded with light.

"I thought my epiphany with Bartolomeo was the highlight, but the hooded figure was just as powerful."

Your epiphany, as you call it, is the centerpiece of all realizations— the opposite of the separateness we were talking about. All is one. By itself, it's just words. When you assimilate it as you did, that's when you take its power into your life. Now the feeling is still very new to you, but as you go on, you will see its truth everywhere you cast your eyes. The fact that you are one with all things changes forever the fundamental character of your life. You will love everything and everyone as you love yourself. And you will love yourself as you love God.

"It was the guides who taught me that the universe sustains me and guides me from within."

I can hear that you are just mouthing the words. Even though you may feel their meaning, you haven't yet taken them into yourself. Is that not so?

Daniel nodded.

Feel what it means! the snake urged. *That the power and purpose of the universe fills you with life and guides your being. What could be more assuring?*

The snake seemed to gaze up into the sky.

We will take a journey that will awaken these truths into the cells of your body.

After a while, the snake gazed at Daniel, its head tilted to one side, questioning. *And what about the presence you met in the chapel?*

"That was just two days ago. It seems like a lifetime."

In many ways, it has been a lifetime.

"Who was he? What was he?"

He is God as initiates first know him.

"Aren't you God?"

Yes. But in this form, I am the god of nations. He is the god of the people.

"Isn't he the one I should be with then?"

The serpent turned away for a moment.

It seems like a paradox. The work to be done affects the outcome of nations. But you, as an individual, are also all the nations. This is a realization for an entirely different era. The Mayan prophecy calls for the work of individuals to transform nations.

The deep whisper receded for a moment and then returned.

The presence in the chapel came to awaken your individuality, an essential step toward the realization of your divinity and your moral imperative. Remember, you are also God. You are here to awaken God within you. Then you and the hundreds of thousands of other Callers will help shape new nations. So you see, I, too, must be part of that transformation.

The idea of shaping nations was utterly incomprehensible to Daniel. The world beyond this place, the world he had left behind, was monstrous. Its corruption against itself was a poison that coursed through nearly all the arteries of its being, spreading death and decay. The scale of its degeneration was beyond imagining. It was a horror.

As if the snake also sensed the enormity of the task that lay ahead, he lowered his eyes to the ground, searching for the thread of a truth.

Do you remember November 9, 1989?

Daniel glanced up into the sky looking for an answer and shook his head. "No, I don't."

It was the day the Berlin wall started to come down.

Daniel's eyes lit up. "What a miracle that was. I remember the celebration a month or so later when, on Christmas Day, Leonard Bernstein led a chorus from Eastern and Western nations in Beethoven's Ninth Symphony. All those nations singing together. I cried."

Exactly! It was a miracle. Do you remember how impossible the world seemed before then? The cold war seemed to permeate the whole world. There was talk of annihilating one another. There seemed to be no other solution. Imagine! But the beliefs that supported that condition were corrupt, and some of them collapsed in on themselves. Overnight, the tensions dissolved.

Unfortunately, only some of the corruption died, and new corruptions were born. The separateness of man from the universe still filled everyone's beliefs, as it does today. There wasn't enough light to overcome the embedded darkness. Today, all those corruptions have aligned against each other, and even against themselves. The scale of corruption has spilled even onto the earth itself and the world is being taken to its darkest place. But the same dynamic that led to the fall of the Berlin wall is at work now, and there will be an opportunity for new miracles to take place.

"On December 21, 2012."

Yes. That's when it begins. But this time, if there are enough Callers to speak the larger truths, all corruption will suffocate under the weight of its own falsehood. It's always the few who have corrupted the lives of the many. All you have to do is look around to see that the world is teeming with innocents. Unfortunately, the forces of the few are deeply rooted and the voice of the weak has been muted. But the strength of the few is man-made. The strength of the humble is divine. On December 21, 2012, there will be an opportunity for the meek to prevail.

Daniel remembered how insurmountable the cold war had seemed. The global situation was so complex and so overwhelming that it appeared certain that the world would come to a terrifying nuclear end. And then, in spite of all the debate, in spite of all the righteous posturing and the dull anxiety that had, for decades, blanketed entire nations, it was all gone in a day—without a single shot fired.

The forces of change are already at work from within. Many enlightened souls are emerging. They shine a light on what wonders may come to be. Man's beliefs shape his destiny. The Callers will help awaken the truths of his being and thereby open the paths of his unfolding.

It seemed such an idyllic outcome. And yet he could clearly see the growing momentum of darkness in the world. As climate change spawned wildfires, tornadoes, hurricanes, and floods; as earthquakes and mudslides turned entire villages into rubble; as political, social, and religious differences gave rise to terrorism, genocide, and war; as the world teetered on the edge of economic chaos, it was not hard to imagine apocalypse in the making. The Maya, however, along with numerous other cultures and disciplines, had somehow discerned the largest cosmic cycles of man's destiny and the forces that surround it. And in those cycles they found, like the pause of a pendulum at its apogee, an opportunity for total change—a second chance for all mankind.

The promise you received the day you died is the promise that awaits everyone. It's the promise of all-consuming love. Do you recall being told that love was the unifying force of the cosmos? Living in that light, here on earth, knowing that, in your deepest essence, you are divine, you will be able to create and receive more love than you could ever imagine.

As if guided by the same hand, the serpent and Daniel both turned to look out at the immense mountain that still seemed close enough to touch. The early sun shone at an angle and the peak cast a long shadow on the clouds behind it. Daniel wondered about all the people below who, on this morning, would look up and see only a heavy gray sky. Though they stood at the base of the volcano, this magnificent peak was lost to them. They lived in a different reality.

Turning back to Daniel, the snake asked, *Do you have any questions?*

Daniel searched himself. "Part of me has a hundred questions and another part of me is at peace."

The serpent cocked its head and seemed very pleased.

That's a perfect response. You are in transition. Those hundred questions will soon dissolve.

Daniel had to push the question out of himself. "How?"

I will guide you through a journey into yourself.

Daniel took a deep breath and looked around. "I'm still afraid," he said. "I can feel that I'm coming closer and closer to the oneness I have wanted all my life. Now, the closer I get, the more I am afraid."

I'm aware. But you are here to realize the greatest transformation of your life. Even we gods would feel apprehensive. I will be with you.

The head of the great serpent curled back on itself toward the center of the ledge.

Sit here within the circle of your centeredness, face the white mountain, and hold the red stone gently in your lap. When you have reached the silence, we will set your intention to own the three truths you have been given. Then we will fulfill the challenge given to you by the hooded god: to take back your life.

Quetzal paused.

It's much more than just taking back your life. It's taking back your power. The snake's head rose and fell slowly, as it observed Daniel.

You can't imagine how great that power is.

There was a long pause.

When you are ready, take yourself into the silence. I will join you when the time is right.

Daniel moved to the middle of the large red circle, picked up the red lava stone, then sat down and folded his legs under him. Cradling the stone in his lap, he took a deep breath and let his eyes fall closed. Morning sun laid its hands on the back of his neck and shoulders, and he allowed its warm comfort to seep down through his body. Cool air brushed the shadow along his cheek and over his eyelids and forehead.

Now he drew his breath in a deep, steady cadence. He could feel anxiety and fear drain down through his extremities and saw it running like a silver river of mercury driven before a great wind, out across the stone ledge. There at the rim, the river pooled for one last time then poured over the edge and out of sight. Soon, these visions faded and his attention followed his breath deep into the expanding awareness of his being. His silent presence—dark, stirring—grew deeper and deeper into the empty stillness. Like a pendulum caught in the rhythm of the universe, his body began to rock slowly back and forth.

A whisper arose through the vast emptiness.

Open your heart.

A long silence returned to fill the space.

We are here to receive the deep realizations of the three cosmic truths.

Again, the soft whisper receded into the silence, as if following the slow, steady rhythm of Daniel's breath.

The truths are all nested within each other and you will experience them as a whole. All is One. You are God's perfect creation. And God fills you like the sun and guides you from within.

Daniel's heart swelled. He had never heard the truths spoken in those words. Nor had they ever been seeded into these deepest parts of himself. He could feel their power take hold within him.

We are here to prepare you to receive your deepest identity. You are divine.

The stillness Daniel had created only moments earlier now brimmed with a warmth that filled his entire body.

Allow your feelings to become the sweetness of honey.

The whisper merged into the beating of his heart. Peace flowed through him like a lake of gold and the word "God" shimmered over the water. But it was no longer just a word. It was a physical power that embraced him, as if both to awaken and soothe. He had heard the word, used the word a thousand, thousand times. But now, when it came from the serpent's whisper deep within him, it created dancing waves of warm colors that wanted to flood out over the earth and envelop it in its light.

We are here to join you with all of creation—to make you and all experience one. This is a journey to reach the largest possible realization of yourself—a journey of your heart, a journey of feeling and consciousness.

The whispered voice now rose and fell in perfect unison with Daniel's breathing and filled the vast space that began to expand within him.

Bring the openness of your heart to receive your wholeness, to feel your presence far beyond the edge of your self—here, on this mountain, heaved up from the deepest parts of the earth. Sit in this first warmth of morning, breaking through the distances that lie around us. Breathe in the freshness of the scented air. Feel the energy of the earth beneath you—alive, stirring with forces of unimaginable magnitude, the planet slowly turning into the sun. This great expanse is all you! Rising from the very core, you are the granite, and the glint of minerals, and the soft whisper of the wind. Feel yourself as the mountain; feel your power and your majesty; feel the fire of your beginning; feel the eons that have passed through you. Remember the wondrous scenes of open sky that have appeared above you.

The voice took a breath and held a long pause.

Now you will leave your body and come with me into the heavens.

In an instant, Daniel felt his awareness depart his body and rise up from the ledge. He looked down and saw he had no arms or hands, no legs, no body. Looking back, he saw himself still sitting in the red circle with his eyes closed, and Quetzal lying long and luxurious in the sun. He felt himself rise up through the clouds and into the heavens. Streaking past the shell of light that enveloped the earth, he emerged into darkness, distant from the shrinking sun, far into a void dotted with star clusters and whirling galaxies. Soon the voice joined him.

Even out of your body, the place we are going to is too far away. From here you must travel with your mind. We are going to an instant some thirteen billion light years away, the center of a cosmos that no longer has a center.

Daniel felt his awareness shift to yet another plane, a dimension that had no distance, where time compressed into a realm of infinite possibilities.

Come with me to a moment when all the cosmos was symmetry in equilibrium. It is an infinitely small point of infinite potential.

Daniel could see the invisible point of nothingness and he thought he could feel its symmetry.

Everything in the cosmos today was born here. Even God. From here came the gasses, the clouds, galaxies, stars, and planets beyond counting. And from within that fire came life. If you look, you can see it all unfolding.

Daniel saw the fiery violence that tore away from where he watched. He saw it explode from blinding white heat into vortices of swirling gasses, and within that chaos he saw the hand of God already creating order.

"How is it that I can see these things?" he asked.

In the presence of all of this, that's not a question I expected, responded the voice with a sound of surprise. *But it's a good question. You can see it because this and all the history of the cosmos is written within you. In your cells and far into your unconscious. You have inherited the memory of everything from this point of your beginning going outward. After all, this is where you came from. If you look closely, you will also see that every detail has unfolded perfectly. And you are the creation of that perfection.*

The voice paused.

But your question tells me that this experience has not touched you deep within.

Daniel searched his awareness. "I can see all these things and I can feel their meaning, but I think it's too much to absorb all at once. I mean, look at all this! An entire universe rushing away creating itself. With God in there as well!"

Ah, the voice exclaimed. *God is more than "in there." That is God. I realize now that we came here in mind. This is an example of why you must feel the truths and not just know them. You can't learn them with just your mind. They must be awakened from within the all of yourself.*

Come. We will go back to earth to a place where you will feel the power of this experience—the ocean.

Daniel gathered up that part of himself that stretched across the timeless dimension from the center of the universe to the edges of now. He then retreated to his awareness, which awaited him in the void and, turning, saw at an incredible distance the sun and the blue speck of earth. The void receded and the earth neared. Plunging through the atmosphere, he swept over the oceans and around the earth until, beneath him, ran a long rim of rocky coast fringed in white. Like a bird over the land, he turned into the wind and dove downward. He came to stand by the edge of the sea, waves crashing, wind rushing into his face. He was fully aware of all his surroundings—the sun, the sounds of the sea, and the distances that unfolded over the horizon. For long moments, he simply allowed it all to come to him, until the voice arose within him again.

Feel these relentless waves against the shore. This is the force that now sustains you—that embraces you from all directions.

The deep power of the sea swept toward him.

In just moments, he felt the deep power of the sea reaching toward him.

Energy without end, the voice continued, *the movement of consciousness, the vitality of nature itself, manifesting its essence.*

He could feel his body open.

You are the swells of all the earth—breathing, rising, falling.

It was as if all the soul of the earth started to flow through him.

You are the air, the gulls, the grass-crested dunes against the sky. All this fills you and speaks to you with the voice of God from within. God fills you and guides you as he does the birds, the flowers, and the sea. Here, you are the rocks, the lichen, the crashing mountains of incoming sea. And everywhere, the wind . . . the wind . . . the wind.

The words became energy that flowed through his body.

Now come with me inland to a quiet valley in the sun—in an instant his awareness hovered over a lush green valley—*and be in tall grasses, among wildflowers and perfume, and in the warmth of the sun.*

All the peaceful details of this valley manifested around him: tall grass bending before a soft breeze, small yellow butterflies hovering over lavender blossoms, aspens shimmering in the sun, and the warm sweet smell of summer. His awareness settled over a field of flowers and the voice joined him.

What distilled the color of these petals? Their softness? Their shape? What guides their faces to follow the sun? What designed the veined perfection of the dragonfly's wings? This is you, here, born from each other. You, these flowers, the trees, the sun itself are all from the single beginning—a perfect creation.

Once again, Daniel could feel himself merging into his surroundings. He was being guided by a voice that sounded like a gentle breeze through pines, and he felt himself entwined into its softness.

From the beginning, the cosmos has conspired for your wellbeing. It is all you.

He could feel every detail flowing into him, warm, intimate, one.

This is you. Own it!

It seemed the voice had receded for an hour, then finally arose once again.

There is one more place we must go, it said.

Daniel knew instantly where that was—the cave dwellings in the southwest that had spoken to him long, long ago and awakened in him the hunger for wholeness that had driven him to this very moment in his life. It was the immense eagle overhead that cracked open the skies to let him glimpse an eternity he could not hold onto.

Come with me now toward the setting sun and the burning clouds—far around to the canyon's edge and down to the stream.

Daniel saw every feature of the landscape, as if they were being born within him. And in an instant, he knew that this experience would transcend all those that had come before.

It's a place you know well. Here, in the ancient land of your ancestors. Listen to the quiet wind. Feel the spirit all around you—in every detail of its manifestation. Take with you the deepest knowledge of your being—and more. Step across the shadows, beyond the edges of your understanding, to look back upon yourself, as if you were consciousness emerging.

The whisper swept through the canyon.

Allow your awareness to reach its farthest horizons. Carry that presence with you—its origin, its nature, its essence. Receive these truths of your self. Dance with them at the edge of the ecstasy you now feel. Knowing these truths, reach once again for the eternal. It has been there all along—the whisper, the intimacy of the air that embraces and carries you—you are one with it. This is your destination.

You see, you are not alone. Here, vast beyond seeing is your reality, the largest truth of your being. You are the all of creation. Participate in this mystery and linger in the arms of this knowing.

Daniel felt his whole body succumb to the enormity of his experience.

Open to receive everything around you. There is only completeness embraced by the eternal. Come. Own this knowledge. Drink from this stream, now crimson in the setting sun.

Daniel knelt by the stream and drank the cool dark water. Its peace touched every part of his being.

Now all this you will know forever.

THE SERPENT WATCHED DANIEL FOR A LONG WHILE, THEN cautiously moved closer and closer to him, its head rising and falling, its tongue testing the air. When it was satisfied that he was not fully returned, it reared its large head back as if to strike, then continued to rise into the air and into the full light of the sun. As it did so, its body widened in the middle and became flat; the colored feathers turned white like silver. Its head became round and its darting tongue solidified into a beautiful golden beak. Its green eyes turned black like glistening marbles set into the smooth feathers that covered its entire head. Its body, now balanced on the tip of its tail, stretched higher and higher; the flat widening along its breast unfolded into splendid wings that stretched far out beyond the ends of the ledge. With a sound like a large kite catching the wind, its tail burst into a fan of long, pure-white feathers, and the creature was lifted aloft as an enormous white eagle, radiating its own blinding white light. Its layered wings undulated slowly through the air and it floated out over the clouds toward the snow-covered peak. It filled nearly half the sky.

As he emerged from the depths of his meditation, Daniel could see the bird's magnificent light through his closed eyelids and could feel its radiance upon his face. The aura filled and warmed his body. He thought of the last truth: God fills you like the sun and guides you from within.

You may open your eyes when you are ready. The voice seemed to come from far away.

The immense white creature shone like a hundred suns.

After a few moments, Daniel's eyes fluttered partly open, squinting against the dazzling light. There before him, nearly too intense to distinguish, waves of radiance flowed out from the churning wings and away from the bird's great body. They swirled in the air like a sea of luminous energy that washed through his flesh and made him feel radiant as well.

Don't be afraid.

Now the voice swept through him, a vast whisper carried on the wind. Shielding his eyes with his hand, Daniel strained to see the immense white creature that shone like a hundred suns.

"Where is Quetzal?" he asked.

I am the new Quetzal, came the breath, *born from Quetzalcoatl. My plumage, once the crown of nobility, now the light of heaven to show the way. I am the one you have come to see.*

Daniel's body felt as if it had no substance, rather like the warm air itself, rising and falling with the waves of light. The thick clouds that had blanketed the sky over the valley burned away like smoke before the wind, and light from the splendid bird flooded everywhere. The great wings surged through the air, the eyes, the head, the golden beak intent upon the man on the ledge.

You have come a long, long way.

"I feel as if my body has evaporated," Daniel said.

You drank the water from the stream.

"Was that the realization of my divinity? I don't know how it would feel."

You will know soon enough, came the deep whisper.

The words swam through his consciousness. "What more can there be?"

Do you feel empowered? Delivered?

Daniel explored himself. "Yes, in a way," he said.

Would you have come all this way just to feel as you do now?

He didn't know what to say. So many new feelings coursed through him. He had seen the birth of God at the center of the universe. And he had drunk from the stream and was filled with peace. He felt wonderful! Now Quetzal's vagueness once again alarmed him, awakening a deep sense of helplessness that seemed to go back endlessly into the darkness of his beginnings. The words flowed up into him, "I don't know what you ask of me," he said.

The hollowed voice rushed through him. *I feel your aloneness, your helplessness,* it said. *Leave them there on the ledge and come toward me.*

Daniel squinted for long moments into the bright light. "I'm afraid," he said.

Your fear is now only a memory. Look behind you.

Daniel turned and there, at the mouth of the cave, was the thin brown and gray snake, its head raised, ready to strike.

Though he's still a baby, he's one of the most poisonous snakes around. Had he bitten you, you would have died within an hour. And yet you carried him against your body all this way. So what is fear?

He gazed at the small snake, still a safe distance away. He felt suddenly confused that, only yesterday, he had taken up the creature and held it against his warm skin. The snake had even shared his fear. Now it was fear that would keep them apart.

Try to recapture what possessed you when you plucked him from the grass. By some peace instilled within you, by your growing sense of oneness, you were not afraid. You knew there was nothing to be afraid of. You were fearless. You transcended the struggle between nature and yourself.

Daniel could feel the truth of all that Quetzal said, and he tried to hold on to its meaning.

More than that, the voice went on, *your beliefs allowed you to co-create a new and different reality. In that moment, you realized your oneness with God. Your divinity.*

Warm air and white light rushed out from the immense wings of the eagle and washed through his body.

This is truly the taking back of your life. You will never again struggle alone. You will never again be alone. This is the promise of your divinity. But there is one more step to take. Come. We must go to the snow-covered mountain.

Instantly, Daniel realized he had known all along that this is what would be asked of him—to go to the mountain. He had known it the moment he beheld its massive presence yesterday in the setting sun. It beckoned him then and now, through the soothing whisper of Quetzal, it called him again. Maybe he had known it the day he died. Maybe he had known it with Leila. Maybe he had known it from a lifetime long ago. There on the volcano he would find the fulfillment of his journey. And he knew what he must do to go there.

Daniel tucked the red stone back into his pouch and walked to the edge of the massive flat stone. Straight down, through the gleaming brightness, he saw the sheer rock that cut back and disappeared beneath him. Far below, he could see what seemed like a small silver stream that followed the base of the mountain. And there, suspended in the air in front of him, as if all the energy of the universe vibrated before him, he saw a vortex of blinding light. Beyond, the entire snow-covered volcano shimmered in an aura of pink and gold. It seemed to dance toward him then recede, inviting him forward into an infinite blue sky.

He felt the profound and immense truth that lay before him. Like a solid platform born from the deepest surging of the earth and the principles of the universe itself, it rose up to support and sustain his being. Tears of joy streamed down his face. His breath surged through him. Everything in his life until this moment seemed to have arrived through the distorting lens of material man. Now, all that fell away and he saw deeply into the underlying wonder of creation, its waves of energy receding and expanding infinitely in all directions. There was no time. There was only the Now that embraced him and all things. He felt safe.

You will never again struggle alone.

The eagle seemed to cock its head to one side as if to behold Daniel with an all-encompassing love. Its wings swept forward and back, inviting him into itself.

Behold the plane of your divinity, the voice continued. *Come. Trust. Walk in the light.*

For a long while, Daniel gazed through Quetzal to the snow-covered mountain beyond. His heart soared. The snow itself shimmered with energy. Then, without looking down, he stepped off the ledge and into the light.

NOTHING WAS EVER THE SAME AGAIN.

"You have a little over an hour. Dean Holbrook will say a few words, then Dr. Coleman will introduce you. Is there anything I can get you to help you feel at home?"

Daniel shrugged and looked at his wife, Rebecca, to see if there was anything she needed. "May I have another cup of tea?" she asked.

"Right away," the young man said, and closed the door behind himself.

Late afternoon light streamed through the rippled window panes onto shelves of books that lined the walls from floor to ceiling. It felt comforting to stand before the newly lit fire that crackled in the fireplace. Outside, red and yellow leaves of autumn lined quiet student paths.

"I still get nervous before these things," Daniel said.

"You'll do just fine. I realize how much I miss a fire in the fireplace." Rebecca stood up and joined him in front of the fire. She was tall and slender, with green eyes and smartly cut light hair. Originally from the Midwest, she had spent most of her life in New York as a photographer. Now they lived at the edge of the desert among saguaros, immense rocks, and flaming sunsets. They usually traveled for two or three months at a time, during which Daniel spoke before as many groups as he could schedule.

"I don't miss driving in the snow one bit," he said.

There was a knock at the door and the young man poked his head in. "I'm sorry to disturb you, but there is a couple here who say they know you and would like to come in to see you. A Mr. and Mrs. Schneider."

"Schneider?" Daniel asked. "Leila Schneider? What would she be doing here?"

"Would you like me to ask?"

"No. No. I'm sure it's Leila and Karl. Please show them in."

The young man disappeared.

"My God, it's been twelve years since I've seen them," Daniel said. "You've never met them, have you?"

After a few moments the door opened and Leila stepped into the room, smiling. Karl, though now a bit stooped, could still fill a doorway.

"Daniel Bancroft," she said, rushing up to give him a hug. Her hair was all gray, still pulled back in a bun; her eyes were still deep and dark brown. Karl, wearing a dark-blue suit that was too small, patted Daniel on the shoulder.

The young man followed them into the room. "May I offer you some tea?"

"I'd love some," Leila said. "Chamomile, if you have it."

"That's what I'm having," Rebecca said.

"What a wonderful surprise," Daniel exclaimed.

Turning her attention to Rebecca, Leila said, "And you must be the bride."

"I'm afraid that was ten years ago."

"Daniel e-mailed me when you met. He's a lucky man."

Karl leaned forward to shake Rebecca's hand. "I'm Karl Schneider," he said in the raspy, breathy voice Daniel had forgotten.

"Oh, I've heard all about both of you," Rebecca said. "Yes, he *is* a lucky man." They laughed.

"What on earth brings you way up here?"

"Our grandson is a freshman here. We saw in the bulletin that you'd be giving a talk, so we just had to drive up."

Daniel felt a special warm spot in his heart for both of them. "It's good to see you. Here, have a seat."

"I brought you a present," Leila said, handing him a feather. "It's from a mourning dove. I remembered how much you liked them."

Daniel ran his fingers over the soft ribbed texture. "This is wonderful. Thank you." Then it occurred to him to ask, "Have you found any white eagle feathers lately?"

Leila cocked her head. "I didn't know there were white eagles."

"Keep your eyes peeled."

After a while the chatter stopped suddenly and an air of expectation filled the room. "So much has happened," Leila said.

Daniel nodded his head in agreement.

"We last heard from you in Atlanta, but after that the news stopped."

Daniel took a deep breath. "Atlanta was the crucible," he said, tired at the thought. "I lost five jobs in eight years. Full of fear, I kept going back to the only way I knew how to earn a living. It was more of the same, and always in conflict with what I was becoming inside. I finally got the message and said 'No more!'"

"He said he wasn't getting back into the squirrel cage again," Rebecca filled in.

"For six of those years, I didn't know what I was looking for," he said. "I had had an epiphany that I would live into my nineties and that I should lead a spiritual life. But I didn't know what that meant. That's when I started going to Mexico. That's where the guides started to speak to me. Do you remember the guides?"

"Of course I remember the guides. You had more of them than anyone I'd ever known."

"Well, they got to talking. In the beginning, some of them were upset that I had wasted so much of my life doing meaningless things. But the main guide—his name is Melchior—helped keep my attention on the big picture."

"And what is that?" Leila wanted to know.

Karl jumped in. "Saving sheep."

They laughed. "Something like that," Daniel said. "The big picture keeps getting bigger. Right now, it's nothing less than putting an end to what we call the corruption of the world. You, Leila, would probably know about that."

Leila rolled her eyes. "We all do. It's everywhere. Humanity is at the brink."

"Several things are working in our favor," Daniel went on, realizing he was twirling the gray-and-white feather in his fingers. "Global warming is sure to realign the social, economic, and political landscape of the world. And the coming Mayan prophecy of 2012 offers us an opportunity to realign our spiritual landscape. This is mostly what I go around talking about—trying to awaken as many people as I can to their strengths and roles in this transformation."

The young man came in with a tray and two steaming cups of tea, then retreated. Leila gazed off into the fire.

"Daniel's main message is that we are all divine," Rebecca said. "Tell them about the platform."

Karl loosened his tie and Leila turned back to Daniel. "Do you remember your friend Stephen? We met him not long ago at the Oley fair. He came to ask Karl about raising sheep."

"How could I forget him? And Julia."

"He seemed fine. He was glad we knew you, but we never mentioned his wife, or the remote visitation you had with them."

"That visitation became the proof of practically everything I learned. I kept going back to it as confirmation that we're all connected. I've visited a lot of other people since then, going back to their childhoods and trying to heal them with love." He gazed out the window for a moment. "Some of the scenes I run into are just horrific. Brutality. Incest. Absence. It's no wonder things are the way they are."

Leila nodded slowly. "I know." Then, glancing toward Rebecca, she said, "But what's this about a platform?"

"I had an incredible experience in Mexico. I went to the ledge of Quetzal," he told her.

"I've heard of this," Leila interrupted.

"It turns out that Quetzal is the incarnation of the Mexican god Quetzalcoatl for the coming world cycle. Not a feathered serpent, but a gleaming white eagle the size of the sky."

"That's why you asked if I'd seen any white eagles," Leila said.

Daniel smiled and nodded. "Anyway, the best way I can describe my experience with Quetzal is that I was asked to sacrifice my life. To surrender to a much larger reality. In doing so, I saw this immense platform of energy stretching out before me, and I knew that, no matter what I did, that platform would support me. It was like stepping onto a new dimensional plane that was both firm and like a translucent membrane at the same time. I just floated there, unharmed. Fear was simply swept away. I felt a wonderful mixture of love, compassion, and gratitude. It was both sweet and powerful. It made me cry, but I felt safe. I realized it was God—the way the universe is—and that it had always been there and would always be there, provided I *believed* it was there. Not just for me, but for everyone. I'm on the platform now, and I'll be on the platform when I go to speak."

"I saw that you were different the minute I walked in the door," Karl said. "You're not the same Daniel who sat at our kitchen table."

"He was a totally different person when he came back from Mexico," Rebecca said. "I was a little frightened at first. It took some getting used to."

"It's true," Leila agreed. "You seem much more complete and serene. Larger. Confident."

Daniel tried to accept the compliments, if indeed they were compliments. It had been a year now since he came back from Mexico and he was still discovering new facets of himself. He felt wonderful. Old barriers and beliefs seemed to come down every week, and he could detect aspects of his new self as they emerged. He loved nearly everyone he met, because he saw them as children. But beneath it all, he felt an urgency—an impatience to get on with the work of change. He believed this feeling was the moral imperative of which Quetzalcoatle spoke.

"Getting on the platform is literally a leap of faith," he said. "We manifest God in that leap, and without the leap there can be no God. And it's in the believing that we realize that we ourselves are divine. Some of the words I was given were, 'You'll never again struggle alone.' That's what comes to be when you receive and live your oneness with God. And I've never been alone or helpless since."

"It sounds like a whole new level of existence," Leila said.

"I can't begin to describe it."

"And so we're all supposed to surrender our lives? How do we do that?" Leila asked.

"You have to transcend your primal fear," he replied. "You have to take yourself to the very edge in order to realize that there's something much larger, something much more universal and real beyond. It means letting go of the way you think things should be, in order to 'see' the platform before you. It's there for everyone. And the minute you trust that it's there, you step into your divinity."

"I've had those feelings on the farm," Karl rasped. "There are times when I know everything is just right. The sun, the trees, the land, the sheep. I remember walking into the barn and seeing sunlight coming through the loft window onto the hay. It was just perfect."

"That's why I married you," Leila teased, to relieve a sense of joy and sadness that seemed to rise up in her.

"We have glimpses into ourselves and our relationship with our surroundings," Daniel said. "It's the larger truth of our lives. And there are other instances, when we are totally helpless and in crisis, when we get a chance to see these larger truths. In those moments of despair, we're invited onto the platform. 'Let go,' it says. 'Everything will be all right.'"

Leila tried to collect her thoughts. "And so, you go around telling people that they are divine. That's a powerful message."

"There's more to it than that," Daniel said. "Do you remember you thought my life might have to do with the Mayan prophecy?"

"Certainly," Leila responded. "All those guides had to mean something."

"Well, there's more to the Mayan prophecy than we know. When the Mayans were given insight into the cosmos by Kukulkan, their name for Quetzacoatl, they were also promised that, in the alignment of December 21, 2012, there would be an opportunity for all mankind to realize its divinity. It meant transcending duality. All they had to do was believe it. But the priests of that time couldn't agree about the implications of the alignment, much less believe that there was no duality, that they were one with the gods. So the promise of divinity was never recorded. It was essentially lost."

"I'd never heard this before," Leila said, "and I've read practically everything."

"It's the missing heart of the Mayan prophecy," he said. "It's the reason I'm on the road giving talks. In fact next year, I'll be making several pilgrimages down into the Yucatan for further preparation. I'm just waiting for a sign."

For a moment Daniel glanced out at the turning leaves. "But there's a condition," he continued slowly. "When the alignment comes, we can literally co-create a new reality—good or bad—simply by what we believe. The down side is that, if we expect cataclysm and apocalypse as many do, that's what could happen. If not enough of us are pulling the other way, that's when things could get bad. The good news is that, even though this is a prophecy from afar, humanity is deeply involved in its own fate. At the convergence, it will be easier to transcend duality and realize our divinity than it's been in thousands and thousands of years. And one more detail. I'm pretty sure rebirth will come through the Divine Feminine. I had an indescribable encounter with our other half. To this day, I don't know what it meant. But it seems as if only through our feminine side can we embrace our differences to become whole."

Daniel took a deep breath. "So you see, we owe it to ourselves and to all the generations to come to make the right shift. It's a second chance for us all."

Leila sipped the last of her tea; there was a thin trace of tears in her eyes. "I've never heard it described in this way, with this urgency. I mean, I've known all this for years, but I've never stopped to consider how fundamental it is. I feel as if I should have immersed myself in it. Should have lived it. Especially now."

"It's never too late," Daniel said. "Well, I'll take that back. Someday soon it could be."

There was a knock on the door and the young man stepped in. "I'm sorry to break in like this, but, Mr. Bancroft, I think it's time I take you over to the auditorium."

Daniel turned to Leila and Karl. "Can we continue this over dinner? We'll be with several faculty members who would love to meet you."

Karl shrugged. Leila said, "I retired ten years ago, Daniel. I hope we still fit in."

"Are you familiar with the term 'Caller'?" Daniel asked.

Leila cocked her head. "Not that I can remember."

"It's when you make the realization of divinity—yours and others'—your life's work," he said.

Leila nodded, as if recalling the work she had done.

"I'm not sure we can let you retire just yet," Daniel said, spreading his arms. "I owe all this to you."

Leila demurred. "You're the one who came in pain looking for answers," she replied.

The young man led them to the auditorium. "I'll take Mr. Bancroft through this side door, but if you go in through the main entrance you'll find seats reserved for you in the front row."

"We'll have to find our grandson," Leila said.

Rebecca gave Daniel a kiss on the cheek and Leila waved. "Ghee," Rebecca said, their code word for contentment, and Daniel followed the young man into the building.

While the Dean opened with a broad outline of the moral challenges that faced the nation's youth, Daniel descended into a calming meditation. Holding the feather of the mourning dove gently in his fingers, he shed his worldly presence and invoked the light of Quetzal and the firmness of the platform beneath him. With 500 faces lifted toward him, he stepped out onto the platform and said, "I have a vision that you are divine. I am here to ask each of you to awaken that divinity and help change the course of our lives."

Burial Site
Baffles Scientists

Mexico City—A team of archaeologists from the University of Arizona and the National University of Mexico has announced the discovery of an ancient burial site that contains the bones of a 20,000-year-old man along with the remains of a contemporary human being, both embracing the skeleton of a saber-toothed tiger. The site, approximately 250 kilometers east of Mexico City, lies within a ravine near the base of the volcano Orizaba. The remains were uncovered in geological strata dating back to the last ice age.

Acknowledgments

Because even a magical adventure has a basis in fact, I would like to express my gratitude to the following:

Pandit Rajmani Tigunait, and the Himalayan Institute, for teaching me how to meditate; Tricia McCannon for introducing me to my guides; Lynn Learned for her endless generosity and far sightedness; George Rosato and Patricia Harrison for their profound knowledge of publishing and infinite patience sharing that wisdom; Cousin Susan Greene and her husband Arthur Greene for their unconditional support and hospitality; Alan Rinzler for saying "No" to non-fiction; and to the world's ideal editor, Caroline Pincus, whose passion and enthusiasm brought all of the above to fruition.

My deepest thanks to each of you!

About the Author

Photo © *Deborah Whitehouse*

Jock Whitehouse was raised in Mexico where from the age of five he was immersed in its culture, language, and mythology. There he experienced firsthand the strange and mystical practices that are the essence of Mesoamerica's spiritual traditions. After thirty years as a businessman in the United States, he returned to Mexico to find once again the spiritual truths of his life.

Jock lives with his wife Deborah in the central highlands of Mexico. For further information, visit *www.jockwhitehouse.com*.

About the Illustrator

Photograph © Jerry House, Lubbock, Texas

Having worked as an animator for Walt Disney, and with over thirty-five years as a sculptor in bronze, Tom Knapp has to his credit more than twenty life-and heroic-size bronzes in public venues in the United States and around the world, including the Rose Bowl Hall of Fame sculpture commissioned for the front of the Rose Bowl Stadium in Pasadena, CA.

Today, Tom specializes in printmaking and illustration, and is actively represented in more than fifteen major galleries in the United States and Mexico. He and his wife Dorothy live in San Miguel de Allende, Mexico.

Limited edition prints of the wood engraving on the cover of this book are available from the artist at buckhorn56@aol.com.

To Our Readers

Weiser Books, an imprint of Red Wheel/Weiser, publishes books across the entire spectrum of occult and esoteric subjects. Our mission is to publish quality books that will make a difference in people's lives without advocating any one particular path or field of study. We value the integrity, originality, and depth of knowledge of our authors.

Our readers are our most important resource, and we appreciate your input, suggestions, and ideas about what you would like to see published. Please feel free to contact us to request our latest book catalog, or to be added to our mailing list.

Red Wheel/Weiser, LLC
500 Third Street, Suite 230
San Francisco, CA 94107
www.redwheelweiser.com